I0347457

The Importance of Prophet Muhammad in Our Daily Life

Part 1

The Importance of Prophet Muhammad in Our Daily Life

Part 1

By

Shaykh Muhammad Hisham Kabbani

PUBLISHED BY THE
INSTITUTE FOR SPIRITUAL AND CULTURAL ADVANCEMENT

Published and Distributed by:

Institute for Spiritual and Cultural Advancement (ISCA)
17195 Silver Parkway, #201
Fenton, MI 48430 USA
Tel: (888) 278-6624
Fax: (810) 815-0518
Email: staff@naqshbandi.org
Web: http://www.naqshbandi.org

First Edition: September 2013
The Importance of Prophet Muhammad in Our Daily Life, Part 1
ISBN: 978-1-930409-89-7

Library of Congress Cataloging-in-Publication Data

Kabbani, Muhammad Hisham.
The importance of Prophet Muhammad in our daily life / by Shaykh Muhammad Hisham Kabbani.
volumes cm
Includes bibliographical references.
ISBN 978-1-930409-89-7 (alk. paper)
1. Muhammad, Prophet, -632. 2. Naqshabandiyah. I. Title.
BP166.5.K23 2013
297.6'3--dc23
2013013527

PRINTED IN THE UNITED STATES OF AMERICA
15 14 13 12 11 05 06 07 08 09

The author with his beloved spiritual master, His Eminence, Shaykh Muhammad Nazim Adil al-Haqqani in Cyprus. September 2013.

Shaykh Kabbani giving a *suhbah*, an inspired spiritual discourse, in the renowned Naqshbandi *zawiya* in Michigan. In 1990, after thirty years of training he was authorized by his master to teach Islamic spirituality (*tasawwuf*).

Table of Contents

About the Author i
Preface iii
Publisher's Notes v
Masters of the Naqshbandi-Haqqani Golden Chain ix
Recitation before Every Association xi
Speak on Truth and Shari`ah 1
Salawat Nuraniyyah/Salawat Badawi Kubra 7
The Miracle of the 360 Points 9
The Unimaginable Benefits of Salawat 16
Prophetic Teachings of the 360 Points in Humans 18
Who Will See the Prophet in This Life 25
To Recognize One's Blindness 27
Salawat that Immediately Raise You 33
Get the Reward of All Salawat Ever Recited 34
The Dowry of Fatimah az-Zahra 36
How to Amend Heedless Actions 41
The Prophet's Love is with Awliyaullah 45
The Signs of Real Love 47
Salawat Dictated from Prophet 49
Salawat Nuraniyyah/Salawat Badawi Kubra 49
Scientific Truths Rooted in Ahadith 53
Fingers that Bear Witness and Points of the Body 56
Sayyidina Adam Gave Forty Years of His Life 59
Creation of Sayyidina Muhammad's Light 61
Holding One's Fingers in a Specific Way 65
Energy Points in the Human Body as Mentioned by Prophet 66
Giving the Remainder of Your Life to Extend Another's 69
The All-Encompassing Power of the Purest Love 73
Numbers in Islam 76
Familiarity Extinguishes Good Manners 77
Saved from Punishment of the Grave 85
The Angels' Salawat Is Continuous 88
Genuine Inspiration is from Prophet and is Always Clear 95
Islam is Based on Obedience 99
How Shaykh Sharafuddin's Life was Extended 107
Arrogance Generates a Putred Smell 108
Shaykh Zia's Du`a 114

Proof of the Shaykh Giving His Life to Others 117
Verses of Holy Qur'an about Dhikrullah..119
Benefits of Making Salawat on the Prophet 126
Introduction to Sultan adh-Dhikr 129
The Shaykh's Power is not on Our Level..135
The Meaning of Allah's Order, "Obey Those in Authority" 139
Two Types of Authority...141
Islamic Calendar and Holy Days 147
Glossary... 151
Other Publications... 134

About the Author

World-renowned religious scholar Shaykh Muḥammad Hisham Kabbani is featured in the ground-breaking book published by Georgetown University, *The 500 Most Influential Muslims in the World*. For decades, he has promoted traditional Islamic principles of peace, tolerance, love, compassion and brotherhood, while rigorously opposing extremism in all its forms. He hails from a respected family of traditional Islamic scholars, which includes the former head of the Association of Muslim Scholars of Lebanon and the present grand mufti (highest Islamic religious authority) of Lebanon.

Shaykh Kabbani is highly trained, both as a western scientist and as an Islamic scholar. He received a Bachelor's degree in Chemistry and later studied medicine. Under the instruction of Shaykh ʿAbdAllāh ad-Daghestani of Damascus, he holds a degree in Islamic Divine Law. Shaykh Muḥammad Nazim Adil al-Haqqani, world leader of the Naqshbandi-Haqqani Sufi Order, authorized him to teach and counsel students in Sufism.

In his long-standing effort to promote a better understanding of traditional Islam, in February 2010, Shaykh Kabbani hosted HRH Charles, the Prince of Wales at a cultural event at the revered Old Trafford Stadium in Manchester, U.K. He has hosted two international conferences in the U.S., and regional conferences on a host of contemporary issues that attracted moderate Muslim scholars from Asia, the Far East, Middle East, Africa, U.K. and Eastern Europe. His counsel is sought by media outlets academics, policymakers and government leaders.

For thirty years, Shaykh Kabbani has consistently promoted peaceful cooperation among people of all beliefs. Since the early 1990s, he launched numerous endeavors to bring moderate Muslims into the mainstream. Often at great personal risk, he has been instrumental in awakening Muslim social consciousness regarding the religious duty to stand firm against extremism and terrorism, for the benefit of all. His bright, hopeful outlook, with a goal to honor and serve all humanity, has helped millions understand the difference between moderate mainstream Muslims and minority extremist sects.

In the United States, Shaykh Kabbani serves as Chairman, Islamic Supreme Council of America; Founder, Naqshbandi Sufi Order of America; Advisor, World Organization for Resource Development and Education; Chairman, As-*Sunnah* Foundation of America; Founder, *The Muslim Magazine*. In the United Kingdom, Shaykh Kabbani is an advisor to Sufi Muslim Council, which consults to the British government on public policy and social and religious issues.

Other titles by Shaykh Kabbani include: *The Dome of Provisions* (2013), *The Hierarchy of Saints* (2013, also in French), *Healing Verses in the Holy Qur'an and Sunnah* (2013), *Salawāt of Tremendous Blessings* (2012, also in Turkish/Spanish), *The Heavenly Power of Divine Obedience and Gratitude* (2012), *The Sufilive Series* (2010-2012), *The Prohibition of Domestic Violence in Islam* (2011, also in French, Spanish), *At the Feet of My Master* (2010), *The Nine-fold Ascent* (2009), *Banquet for the Soul* (2008), *Illuminations* (2007), *Universe Rising* (2007), *Symphony of Remembrance* (2007), *A Spiritual Commentary on the Chapter of Sincerity* (2006), *The Sufi Science of Self-Realization* (Fons Vitae, 2005), *Keys to the Divine Kingdom* (2005), *Classical Islam and the Naqshbandi Sufi Order* (2004), *The Naqshbandi Sufi Tradition Guidebook* (2004), *The Approach of Armageddon? An Islamic Perspective* (2003), *Encyclopedia of Muḥammad's Women Companions and the Traditions They Related* (1998, with Dr. Laleh Bakhtiar), *Encyclopedia of Islamic Doctrine* (7 vols. 1998), *Angels Unveiled* (1996), *The Naqshbandi Sufi Way* (1995), and *Remembrance of God Liturgy of the Sufi Naqshbandi Masters* (1994).

Preface

This book is based on the *suḥbah,* extemporaneous, divinely inspired discourses, of Shaykh Hisham Kabbani, disciple and representative of the global head of the Naqshbandi-Haqqani Sufi Order, Mawlana Shaykh Nazim Adil al-Haqqani. Their uplifting discourses often include anecdotes of venerable Sufi masters from the renowned Naqshbandi Golden Chain, which dates back to Prophet Muḥammad ﷺ.

The Importance of Prophet Muḥammad in Our Daily Life was compiled from personal notes of the Sufi masters. It features a detailed explanation of how a quarter of the world population views the Prophet and the specific guidance he provided Mankind so they may achieve *al-Maqām al-Ihsān*, the high spiritual state of moral excellence.

This volume includes several powerful supplications taught by Prophet Muḥammad and their secret spiritual knowledge that is hidden in specific formulas handed down over centuries. The recitations in this book are known to remove obstacles and resolve poor health, financial and personal issues, impart goodness and bring peace to one's heart.

These universal lessons are a fine addition to any study of Islam, Prophet Muḥammad, Sufism, Islamic mysticism, spirituality and New Age teachings.

For fifty years, the author has sought to serve his master and promote these ancient Sufi teachings in the best manner. We hope the book you now hold reflects this spirit and opens a door to the glorious, redeeming traditions given us by Prophet Muḥammad, may the peace and blessing of God be upon him.

Publisher's Notes

This book is directed to those familiar with the Sufi Way; however, to accommodate lay readers unfamiliar with Sufi terminology and practices, we have provided English translations of Arabic texts and a comprehensive glossary. Where Arabic terms are crucial to the discussion, we have included transliteration and explanations. For readers familiar with Arabic and Islamic teachings, for further clarity please consult the cited sources.

The original material is based on transcripts of a series of holy gatherings known as *ṣuḥbah,* a divinely inspired talk given by the "Shaykh," a highly trained spiritual guide. To present the authentic flavor of such rare teachings, great care was taken to preserve the speaking styles of both the author and the illustrious shaykhs upon whose notes this book is based.

Translations from Arabic to English pose unique challenges that we have tried our best to make understandable to Western readers. Please note our application of the common Arabic oral tradition of omitting definite articles such as "~~the~~ Prophet" and "~~the~~ Holy Qur'an," as practiced by Muslims around the world as intimate references.

We apply contemporary American English publishing standards and italicize foreign proper nouns (*Fātiḥah, Quṭb az-Zamān, Rasūlullāh, Sūratu 'n-Naml),* but not commonly known foreign-language nouns (jihād, Qur'an, shaykh) unless they appear in transliterations.

Quotes from the Holy Qur'an and Holy Traditions of Prophet Muḥammad are offset, italicized and cited.

The pronoun "they" is frequently used by Sufi guides to reference heavenly beings and holy souls who support them and give them orders, a usage that appears throughout this book. Where gender-specific pronouns such as "he" and "him" are applied in a general sense, no discrimination is intended towards women, upon whom The Almighty bestowed great honor.

Islamic teachings are primarily based on four sources, in this order:

- **Holy Qur'an**: the Islamic holy book of divine revelation (God's Word) granted to Prophet Muḥammad. Reference to Holy Qur'an appears as "4:12," which indicates "Chapter 4, Verse 12."

- ***Sunnah***: holy traditions of Prophet Muḥammad ﷺ; the systematic recording of his words and actions that comprise the *ḥadīth*. For fifteen centuries, Islam has applied a strict, highly technical standard, rating each narration in terms of its authenticity and categorizing its "transmission." As this book is not highly technical, we simplified the reporting of *ḥadīth*, but included the narrator and source texts to support the discussion at hand.
- ***Ijma'***: The adherence, or agreement of the experts of independent reasoning *(āhl al-ijtihād)* to the conclusions of a given ruling pertaining to what is permitted and what is forbidden after the passing of the Prophet, Peace be upon him, as well as the agreement of the Community of Muslims concerning what is obligatorily known of the religion with its decisive proofs. Perhaps a clearer statement of this principle is, "We do not separate (in belief and practice) from the largest group of the Muslims."
- **Legal Rulings:** highly trained Islamic scholars form legal rulings from their interpretation of the Qur'an and the *Sunnah*, known as *ijtihād*. Such rulings are intended to provide Muslims an Islamic context regarding contemporary social norms. In theological terms, scholars who form legal opinions have completed many years of rigorous training and possess degrees similar to a doctorate in divinity in Islamic knowledge, or in legal terms, hold the status of a high court or supreme court judge, or higher.

The following universally recognized symbols have been respectfully included in this work. While they may seem tedious, they are deeply appreciated by a vast majority of our readers.

ﷻ *Subḥānahu wa Taʿalā* (may His Glory be Exalted), recited after the name "Allāh" and any of the Islamic names of God.

ﷺ *ṢallAllāhu ʿalayhi wa sallam* (God's blessings and greetings of peace be upon him), recited after the holy name of Prophet Muḥammad.

عليه السلام *ʿAlayhi ʿs-salām* (peace be upon him/her), recited after holy names of other prophets, names of Prophet Muḥammad's relatives, the pure and virtuous women in Islam, and angels.

ﷺ/ﷺ *RaḍīAllāhu ʿanh(um)* (may God be pleased with him/her), recited after the holy names of Companions of Prophet Muḥammad; plural: *raḍīAllāhu ʿanhum.*

ق represents *QaddasAllāhu sirrah* (may God sanctify his secret), recited after names of saints.

Transliteration

Transliteration from Arabic to English poses challenges. To show respect, Muslims often capitalize nouns which, in English, appear in lowercase.

To facilitate authentic pronunciation of names, places and terms, use the following key:

Symbol	Transliteration	Symbol	Transliteration	Vowels: Long	
ء	ʻ	ط	ṭ	آ ى	ā
ب	b	ظ	Σ	و	ū
ت	t	ع	¿	ي	ī
ث	th	غ	gh	Short	
ج	j	ف	f	َ	a
ح	ħ	ق	q	ُ	u
خ	kh	ك	k	ِ	i
د	d	ل	l		
ذ	dh	م	m		
ر	r	ن	n		
ز	z	ه	h		
س	s	و	w		
ش	sh	ي	y		
ص	š	ة	ah; at		
ض	ļ	ال	al-/'l-		

Masters of the Naqshbandi-Haqqani Golden Chain

May Allāh ﷻ preserve their secrets.

1. Prophet Muḥammad ibn ʿAbdAllāh ﷺ
2. Abū Bakr as-Ṣiddīq ق
3. Salmān al-Farsi ق
4. Qasim bin Muḥammad bin Abū Bakr ق
5. Jafar aṣ-Ṣādiq ق
6. Tayfur Abū Yazīd al-Bistāmi ق
7. AbūlHassan ʿAlī al-Kharqani ق
8. Abū ʿAlī al-Farmadi ق
9. Abū Yaqūb Yusuf al-Hamadani ق
10. AbūlAbbas, al-Khiḍr ق
11. ʿAbdul Khāliq al-Ghujdawani ق
12. Arif ar-Riwakri ق
13. Khwaja Maḥmūd al-Anjir al-Faghnawi ق
14. ʿAlī ar-Ramitani ق
15. Muḥammad Baba as-Samasi ق
16. as-Sayyid Amir Kulal ق
17. Muḥammad Bahaʿuddin Shah Naqshband ق
18. Alaʿuddin al-Bukhāri al-Attar ق
19. Yaqūb al-Charkhi ق
20. Ubaydullāh al-Aḥrar ق
21. Muḥammad az-Zahid ق
22. Darwish Muḥammad ق
23. Muḥammad Khwaja al-Amkanaki ق
24. Muḥammad al-Baqi billāh ق
25. Aḥmad al-Farūqi as-Sirhindi ق
26. Muḥammad al-Masum ق
27. Muḥammad Sayfuddin al-Farūqi al-Mujaddidi ق
28. as-Sayyid Nūr Muḥammad al-Badawani ق
29. Shamsuddin Habib Allāh ق
30. ʿAbdAllāh ad-Dahlawi ق
31. Khālid al-Baghdādī ق
32. Ismail Muḥammad ash-Shirwāni ق
33. Khas Muḥammad Shirwāni ق
34. Muḥammad Effendi al-Yaraghi ق
35. Jamāluddin al-Ghumuqi al-Ḥusayni ق
36. Abū Aḥmad as-Sughuri ق
37. Abū Muḥammad al-Madani ق
38. Sharafuddīn ad-Daghestāni ق
39. ʿAbdAllāh al-Faʿiz ad-Daghestāni
40. Muḥammad Nazim Adil al-Haqqani ق

Recitation before Every Association

بسم الله الرحمن الرحيم

Aʿūdhu billāhi min ash-Shayṭān ir-rajīm.
Bismillāhi' r-Raḥmāni 'r-Raḥīm.
Nawaytu 'l-arbāʿīn, nawaytu 'l-ʿitikāf,
nawaytu'l-khalwah, nawaytu 'l-ʿuzlah,
nawaytu 'r-riyāḍa, nawaytu 's-sulūk,
lillāhi Taʿalā fī hādhā 'l-masjid.

Atiʿūllāha wa atiʿ ūr-Rasūla
wa ūli'l-amri minkum.

I seek refuge in Allāh from Satan, the rejected.
In the Name of Allāh, the Merciful,
the Compassionate.
I intend the forty (days of seclusion);
I intend seclusion in the mosque,
I intend seclusion, I intend isolation,
I intend discipline (of the ego); I intend to travel
in God's Path for the sake of God,
in this mosque.

Obey Allāh, obey the Prophet,
and obey those in authority among you.
Sūratu 'n-Nisā (The Women), 4:59

Speak on Truth and Shari`ah

A'ūdhu billāhi min ash-Shayṭāni 'r-rajīm. Bismillāhi' r-Raḥmāni 'r-Raḥīm.
Nawaytu 'l-arbā'īn, nawaytu 'l-'itikāf, nawaytu'l-khalwah, nawaytu 'l-'uzlah,
nawaytu 'r-riyāḍa, nawaytu 's-sulūk, lillāhi Ta'alā fī hādhā 'l-masjid.
Atī'ūllāha wa atī'ū 'r-Rasūla wa ūlī 'l-amri minkum.
Obey Allāh, obey the Prophet, and obey those in authority among you. (4:59)

Dastūr, madad yā Sulṭān al-Awlīyā, Mawlana Shaykh Nazim al-Haqqani ق.
Dastūr, madad yā Sulṭān al-Awlīyā, Mawlana Shaykh 'AbdAllāh ad-Daghestani ق.

If time permits, a few words after the *dhikr* are necessary. We do not say that Allāh ﷻ "chose" Sayyīdinā Muḥammad ﷺ, because that is to imply there were many choices from which to choose. Allāh ﷻ created him and dressed him with the Eternal Light of the Beautiful Names and Attributes of Allāh! He dressed His Prophet ﷺ and by Allāh's ﷻ order the Prophet ﷺ dressed all the prophets عليهم السلام with these Lights, and prophets dressed all the *awlīyāullāh* ق who are standing at their threshold at their feet.

Some ask, how do you recognize *awlīyāullāh*? You know them from these Lights they are dressed with, and we know that, but if you don't give evidence and just throw words in the air, talking about "70,000 blessings" and "70,000 dresses" without giving real evidence, they will ask from where are you bringing that. I never heard Grandshaykh, may Allāh bless his soul, say "70,000" except on one occasion, when he said, "*Majlis adh-Dhikr* (like this *dhikr*) for the love of Allāh ﷻ and His Prophet ﷺ and for remembering Allāh's Name will intercede for seventy *majlis*'." It will take away the sins of seventy bad associations, not 70,000!

But in any case, whatever it is—70,000, 70 or 7,000—we have to give the evidence, which Ibn 'Abbas رضي الله عنه wrote in his *Tafsīr Sūrat al-'Arāf*:

> When Sayyīdinā Musa عليه السلام asked to see Allāh ﷻ, Allāh said to him, "Look at the mountain; when I manifest My Beautiful Names and Attributes you will see Me and if not, you will not see Me." So when Allāh ﷻ manifested His Beautiful Names and Attributes on the mountain, the mountain shattered to powder and Sayyīdinā Musa عليه السلام fainted, and when he woke up he saw (as mentioned by Ibn Abbas), 124,000 prophets.

That number comes from Ibn ʿAbbas's *tafsīr*. The *awlīyāullāh* are on the threshold of 124,000 prophets, so there are 124,000 *awlīyā*. Now we are living in this world between people and when we see something wrong, according to Islamic Shariʿah you have to say, "This is wrong," otherwise you will carry the *wizra*, burden of that as a partner in that wrong.

وَأمَرُوا بِالْمَعْرُوفِ وَنَهَوْا عَنِ الْمُنكَرِ

W 'amarū bi 'l-maʿrūf wa nahaw ʿani 'l-munkar.

And enjoin what is right and forbid what is wrong. (Sūrat al-*Hajj*, 22:41)

So if you see something wrong you say, "This is wrong," you speak out, and then they can correct themselves, and if you see something good, you say, "This is good." And the evidence is the *ḥadīth* of the Prophet ﷺ:

تعرض علي أعمال أمتي

Tuʿradu ʿalayya ʿamāl ummatī.

The deeds of the ummah are presented to me.

SubḥānAllāh, look at the power that Allāh ﷻ gave to Prophet ﷺ! In twenty-four hours, the Prophet ﷺ sees the whole *ummah,* not just one person or a few people but the entire *ummah*! So however many mistakes we make, the Prophet ﷺ is observing and taking the burden away. So our duty is to be realistic. When we speak or give a speech, don't try to come to me and speak from above the ceiling, throwing words, *shatahāt,* something that people cannot understand! Sayyīdinā ʿAbdul Qadir Jilani ﷺ said, "If you see someone flying, then know that is Shayṭan," because a scholar will not fly in the air; rather, he will do things that are realistic. So don't throw words and put things that are not realistic.

Ṭarīqah is based on Shariʿah, not on something we hear about from here and there, so you don't have to go too much into Shariʿah or too much into Haqiqat and spiritual realities. No, you have to build the airplane in order to fly; you cannot fly with half an airplane, you need two wings! Did you ever see a bird flying with one wing? How are you flying above *Qāba Qawsayni aw Adnā* and explaining so high about The Essence, *Dhāt al-Buht,* and that Prophet ﷺ is the Essence? How? No one knows the Essence of Allāh ﷻ, not even the Prophet ﷺ; he ﷺ only knows what Allāh ﷻ gave him to know! People know that, so don't speak too high, about flying above *Qāba Qawsayni aw Adnā* or people will get confused. You must build the structure because a bird with one wing will not fly. Without Shariʿah, one wing, and Haqiqat, the other wing, you cannot take off in flight. But you dropped one and mentioned one, that doesn't work.

All of us and everyone who are following *mashaykh* from any *ṭarīqat*, we are not speaking on any one *ṭarīqat* but we are speaking in general, so don't come and say, "Naqshbandi is the best and the others are bad," because people don't like that. Be fair: there are 124,000 *awlīyā,* and everyone in his *ṭarīqah* says, "My shaykh is *Sulṭān al-Awlīyā,*" so don't create confusion and make people run away! We never heard from Grandshaykh ق that he is *Sulṭān al-Awlīyā* and we never heard him say Shaykh Sharafuddin ق is *Sulṭān al-Awlīyā,* and we never heard Mawlana Shaykh ق say that he is *Sulṭān al-Awlīyā*! We believe he is, but don't put words in his mouth that will backfire against the Naqshbandi Ṭarīqat. Don't let people say one (confrontational) word, because of many representatives speak high above the ceiling and above *Qāba Qawsayni aw Adnā* or people will ask, "How did you speak about *Qāba Qawsayni aw Adnā*? Do you know it/see it?" Then how can you speak about it? You cannot, because you have to be there, so keep your level!

I am not saying that Allāh ﷻ didn't say in Holy Qur'an:

وَفَوْقَ كُلِّ ذِي عِلْمٍ عَلِيمٌ

Fawqa kulli dhi ʿilmin ʿalīm.

Above every knower is a (higher) knower. (Sūrah Yusuf, 12:76)

We respect every knower and Gnostic, but the Gnostic has *adab.* In one lecture in Cyprus they said, "If there is a stone in the street, what do you have to do? You have to take it away." And Mawlana Shaykh Nazim ق taught us not to push it with your feet but take it with your hands and put it aside. It means *imatat al-adha min at-tarīq,* "to remove the harmful thing from the way is from faith" as it might harm you and break your neck, so you are responsible to remove it and that is Shariʿah.

And if a stone that is a human being is blocking the way of people, then what do you do? You remove him or else you are responsible! Why aren't you removing these harmful stones, when Islam teaches to take away the stone that is harmful? But you are saying, "These are good people, we have to keep them there." Remove them with discipline, not with your feet but with your hands, and then if you cannot move them with your hands, then what did the Prophet ﷺ say? "Move them with your tongue."

> *Man ra'a munkaran fal-yughayyiruh bI-yadih fa in lam yastatʿi fa-bi lisānihi wa in lam yastatʿi fa bi 'l-qalbi wa dhalika adʿafu 'l-imān.*
>
> *Whoever sees a wrong, try to change it with your hand; if you are unable, then try to change it with your tongue; if you cannot, then change it with your heart, and this is the lowest level of imān.* (Muslim)

Say, "This is harmful, take him out!" and if you cannot, then (do it) by your heart: raise your hands and say, "*Yā Rabbī*, take them away!" and this is the least of Imān. So if by hand and by tongue we cannot because they are glued like super-glue, so then make *duʿa*. But to come and pet them, praise them and give them support when you know they are wrong, you are going to be in a problem that is not nice. In Arabic we say *massah juh*, "kiss their ass." For what? What is the benefit? Say the truth! Many times you said the truth between you and me. Why are you hiding it?

Last Friday when Mawlana Shaykh Nazim appeared from his window, he was not able to go to the window but they forced him, to say "hello" to the people, and he fell down! He was so tired they had to carry him to the bed, and for what? Only for those people to show from the window that they are behind him. I don't understand.

So our *ṭarīqah* is based on discipline and discipline is to say what is truth and forbid what is bad. You cannot hide what is bad by praising it! If you want to hide it, hide it, it is okay, because you don't want to backbite or spread rumors, but don't say the opposite to thousands around the world and make these (devil) people angels coming from Heaven! What are you benefitting? Nothing. So we have to be realistic in whatever we say and we speak. If we don't bring evidence from Holy Qur'an and from *Holy Ḥadīth*, our words will be rejected.

ʿ*Ulama* are watching what people are speaking on the Internet and scholars are watching; don't say, "There are no more scholars that understand anything from spirituality." No, there are many scholars around the world who are Sufi, are there not? They know theories and they can give you knowledge as much as you like, but the most important is the experience, so with theory is experience. Also, with Islamic Shariʿah you cannot take away spirituality and leave Shariʿah. We know that Grandshaykh ق only gave *baya'* to two, because *awlīyā* do not give authority unless the person is firmly based in Shariʿah and says words that fit in its place, so that they will not make any mistake.

Fa as-sufiyūn al-mukhlisūn maʿ Allāh fī kulla harakāt wa sakanāt.

The truthful Sufis with Allāh are truthful in every movement and in every moment of their lives.

With Allāh ﷻ, to be in the category of *Sādiqūn,* the Truthful, they must be truthful in every moment of their lives, in their outside physical appearances, *zhawāhirihim,* and in their *bātin,* the spiritual appearances. These are the Perfect Ones that you have to follow, these are the ones who reached and won the perfect *ittibaʿ*, obedience to the Prophet ﷺ, and they kept the Shariʿah as it should be, strong.

So *awlīyāullāh* show patience, patience, patience, but at the end, if someone is not accepting and listening, what do they have to do? They have to tell that person, "This is not acceptable." And that is why Mawlana Shaykh Nazim said, "I must have complete Shariʿah in my home," and he said what he said because they cannot come against Shariʿah; they are patient (up to a point), but they will not allow.

Imam Ghazali ؓ said, "The *murīd* who has a teacher must follow him and who has no shaykh, Shayṭan will take him to disaster."

Abu Yazid al-Bistami ؓ said, "Who has no shaykh, his shaykh is Shayṭan!"

That is what we have to be very careful about in our daily life with our *shuyūkh,* to be truthful in presenting to them. Like yesterday I was watching someone giving a speech and I didn't hear anything from him except speaking about Shariʿah and *Haqā'iq,* realities, and then he said, "We are Muslim and if they don't accept us, we must take the sword!" You cannot say these things; this is against Islam! So we have to be very careful of what we are saying.

May Allāh forgive us and bless us.

There is something about *dhikrullāh* that I like to mention. *Awlīyāullāh* have visions and Allāh ﷻ opened their eyes, as mentioned in the *Holy Ḥadīth* of the Prophet ﷺ, *Ḥadīth Qudsī,* that no one can reject as it is a type of revelation in *ḥadīth*:

عن أبي هريرة قال قال رسول الله صلى الله عليه وسلم إن الله قال من عادى لي وليا فقد آذنته بالحرب وما تقرب إلي عبدي بشيء أحب إلي مما افترضت عليه وما يزال عبدي يتقرب إلي بالنوافل حتى أحبه فإذا أحببته كنت سمعه الذي يسمع به وبصره الذي يبصر به ويده التي يبطش بها ورجله التي يمشي بها وإن سألني لأعطينه ولئن استعاذني لأعيذنه وما ترددت عن شيء أنا فاعله ترددي عن نفس المؤمن يكره الموت وأنا أكره مساءته ولا يزال عبدي يتقرب إلي بالنوافل حتى أحبه، فإذا أحببته كنت سمعه الذي يسمع به وبصره الذي يبصر به، ويده التي يبطش بها ورجله التي يمشي بها،

Man ʿada lī waliyan ādhantahu bi 'l-harb wa mā taqarraba ilayya ʿabdī bi-shayyin ahabba ilayya mimmā aftaradtu ʿalayhi wa mā yazālu ʿabdī yataqarabu ilayya bi' n-nawāfil hatta uhibbah. Fa idhā ahbābtahu kuntu samaʿuhulladhī yasmaʿu bihi wa basarahulladhī yubsiru bihi, wa yadahulladhī yabtishu bihā wa rijlahullatī yamshī bihā.

My servant does not cease to approach Me through voluntary worship until I will love him. When I love him, I will become the ears with which he hears, the eyes with which he sees, the hand with which he acts, and the legs with which he walks (and other versions include, "and the tongue with which he speaks.").

(*Ḥadīth Qudsī,* Bukhari)

They can see visions, or dreams. And it is said that Sidi al-Telmesany ق read *Dalāʾil al-Khayrāt*. In our *ṭarīqah*, we are ordered to read one *juz'u* of Holy Qur'an and one *hizb* of *Dalāʾil al-Khayrāt* daily. And he said that shaykh Muḥammad Talmaysani ق read *Dalāʾil al-Khayrāt* 100,000 times and he saw the Prophet ﷺ in the dream. So don't talk about *Qāba Qawsayni aw Adnā* or about love and respect, but give people teaching as that is what they need. And the Prophet ﷺ came to him in the dream and said to him, "If you read the recitation that Aḥmad al-Badawi ق reads every day, it would be as if you read *Dalāʾil al-Khayrāt* 800,000 times!"

To have read it 100,000 times Muḥammad al-Talmaysani had to read it a thousand times every day, is it not? Or is it eighty times? Calculate it later! But the Prophet ﷺ is saying to Muḥammad al-Talmaysani that if you read the *du'a* of Shaykh Aḥmad al-Badawi ؓ you would get the reward of reading *Dalā'il al-Khayrāt* 800,000 times:

Salawat Nuraniyyah/Salawat Badawi Kubra

اَللّٰهُمَّ صَلِّ وَسَلِّمْ وَبَارِكْ عَلَى سَيِّدِنَا وَمَوْلاَنَا مُحَمَّدٍ شَجَرَةِ الاَصْلِ النُّوْرَانِيَّةِ، وَلَمْعَةِ
الْقَبْضَةِ الرَّحْمَانِيَّةِ، وَأَفْضَلِ الْخَلِيْقَةِ الاِنْسَانِيَّةِ، وَأَشْرَفِ الصُّوْرَةِ الْجِسْمَانِيَّةِ، وَمَعْدِنِ
الاَسْرَارِ الرَّبَّانِيَّةِ، وَخَزَائِنِ الْعُلُوْمِ الاِصْطِفَائِيَّةِ، صَاحِبِ الْقَبْضَةِ الاَصْلِيَّةِ، وَالْبَهْجَةِ
السَّنِيَّةِ، وَالرُّتْبَةِ الْعَلِيَّةِ، مَنِ انْدَرَجَتِ النَّبِيُّوْنَ تَحْتَ لِوَائِهِ، فَهُمْ مِنْهُ وَاِلَيْهِ، وَصَلِّ وَسَلِّمْ
وَبَارِكْ عَلَيْهِ وَعَلَى آلِهِ وَصَحْبِهِ عَدَدَ مَاخَلَقْتَ، وَرَزَقْتَ وَأَمَتَّ وَأَحْيَيْتَ اِلَى يَوْمِ تَبْعَثُ
مَنْ أَفْنَيْتَ، وَسَلِّمْ تَسْلِيْمًاكَثِيْرًا وَالْحَمْدُ لِلّٰهِ رَبِّ الْعَالَمِيْنَ.

Allāhumma salli wa sallim wa bārik 'ala Sayyīdinā wa Mawlana Muḥammadin shajarati 'l-aslin nūrāniyyati wa lam'atil qabdati 'r-raḥmāniyyati wa afdali 'l-khalīqati 'l-insāniyyati wa ashrafi 's-sūrati 'l-jismāniyyati wa m'adini 'l-asrāri 'r-rabbanīyyati wa khazāini 'l 'ulūmi 'l-istifāiyyati, sāḥibi 'l-qabdati 'l-asliyya wa 'l-bahjati 's-saniyya wa 'r-rutbati 'l-'aliyya, manin darajati 'n-nabiyyūna tahtali wāihi, fahum minhu wa ilayhi, wa salli wa sallim wa bārik 'alayhi wa 'ala ālihi wa sāḥbihi 'adada mā khalaqta wa razaqta wa amatta wa ahyayta ilā yawmi tab'athu man afnayta wa sallim taslīman kathīra wa 'l-hamdulillāhi rabbi 'l-'alamīn.

O Allāh! Bless, greet and sanctify our master and liegelord Muḥammad ﷺ, the Tree of Original Light, the Sparkle of the Handful of Divine Mercy, the Best of All Humankind, the Noblest of Physical Frames, the Vessel of the Lord's Secrets and Storehouse of the Sciences of the Elect, the Possessor of the Original Divine Grasp, Resplendent Grace, and Uppermost Rank, under whose flag line up all the Prophets, so that they are from him and point to him. Bless, greet and sanctify him and his Family and Companions, to the number of all that You have ever created, sustained, caused to die and caused to live again, to the Day You resurrect those You reduced to dust, and greet him with an abundant and endless greeting. Glory and praise belong to Allāh, the Lord of the Worlds!

Now we are rewarded for having read *Dalāʿil al-Khayrāt* 800,000 times! Such teachings make us run after this *ṭarīqah* for the good tidings and what we must do to make progress, and they are so simple. You see how much time Sayyid Muḥammad al-Talmaysani ﷺ spent to read that and the Prophet ﷺ said to him, "Read the recitation of Sayyīdinā Aḥmad al-Badawi ق, that in one recitation covers *Dalāʿil al-Khayrāt* 800,000 times." *Allāhu Akbar!*

Next time we will mention some recitations we can read in order to see the Prophet ﷺ, *inshā'Allāh. Ila hadrati 'n-nabi, salla-Allāhu ʿalayhi wa sallam wa ālihi wa sāḥbihi 'l-kirām wa ila arwāhi al-a'immati'l-arbaʿ wa ila arwāhi ābā'inā wa umahātinā wa ustādhi wa ustādhi ustādhinā wa sa'iri sādātinā was-siddīqīna, al-Fātiḥah.*

By the way, no one in the Naqshbandi Order is involved in Buddhist training for different points! We don't want to discuss these issues because we left it behind us.

May Allāh ﷻ forgive us and may Allāh ﷻ bless us.

Wa min Allāhi ʿt-tawfiq, bi ḥurmati ʿl-ḥabīb, bi ḥurmati ʿl-Fātiḥah.

And with Allāh is success. For the sake of the Beloved, for his sake we recite the opening chapter of Holy Qur'an.

The Miracle of the 360 Points

Aʿūdhu billāhi min ash-Shayṭāni 'r-rajīm. Bismillāhi' r-Raḥmāni 'r-Raḥīm.
Nawaytu 'l-arbāʿīn, nawaytu 'l-ʿitikāf, nawaytu'l-khalwah, nawaytu 'l-ʿuzlah,
nawaytu 'r-riyāḍa, nawaytu 's-sulūk, lillāhi Taʿalā fī hādhā 'l-masjid.
Atīʿūllāha wa atīʿū 'r-Rasūla wa ūlī 'l-amri minkum.
Obey Allāh, obey the Prophet, and obey those in authority among you. (4:59)

Dastūr, madad yā Sulṭān al-Awlīyā, Mawlana Shaykh Nazim al-Haqqani ق.
Dastūr, madad yā Sulṭān al-Awlīyā, Mawlana Shaykh ʿAbdAllāh ad-Daghestani ق.

Allāh ﷻ said in Holy Qur'an, "Above every knower is a (higher) knower," (12:76) which means above every knowledge is a (higher) knowledge. Therefore, as much as we learn, as Sayyīdinā ʿAlī ؓ said, "Knowledge raises up who is in a low level of knowledge, and when he learns he will be respected and honored by the people around him or from his teachings."

That's why if you teach yourself what the Prophet ﷺ taught the *Saḥābah* ؓ, and what they taught those who came after them, and those who came after them from pious people who taught us raises our level of respect. Someone who doesn't learn has no value in the community and the society.

People today are not only reading books, but they are recording lectures and with technology, knowledge is spreading everywhere. The most important is not the knowledge of Shayṭan, but we are concerned with heavenly knowledge that Prophet ﷺ showed us, and Allāh ﷻ has ordered us to take whatever the Prophet ﷺ gave us.

وَمَا آتَاكُمُ الرَّسُولُ فَخُذُوهُ وَمَا نَهَاكُمْ عَنْهُ فَانتَهُوا

Wa mā ātākumu 'r-rasūlu fakhudhūhu wa mā nahākum ʿanhu fantahū.

Leave what Prophet ﷺ forbade and take what he ordered.

(Sūrat al-Hashr, 59:7)

What did the Prophet ﷺ give us? He gave his life; he gave us hundreds of thousands of *aḥadīth*! How many *aḥadīth* do we know—five, ten or twenty? But if you study and learn the *ḥadīth*, then you will discover that there are hundreds of thousands of *ḥadīth*. Imam Aḥmad bin Hanbal ق said, "I have memorized over 300,000 *aḥadīth*," because in every moment Prophet ﷺ was saying something; he was not sitting quietly with *Saḥābah* ؓ, so for every moment there is a *ḥadīth*. There must be more than 300,000. I heard Grandshaykh, may Allāh bless his soul, say that through the connection that *awliyā* have to the presence of the Prophet ﷺ that more than 700,000 *ḥadīth* have been mentioned!

And you cannot find many of those scholars today, although there are scholars today, but not of such high caliber. What do you think of a scholar who is at the same time a wali? He can ask from the Prophet ﷺ, and many *awliyāullāh* have asked Prophet ﷺ through their dreams about the authenticity of *ḥadīth*. They see Prophet ﷺ in their dreams, so can we say they are lying? What is the evidence to accuse them of lying? Some people can see the Prophet ﷺ in a dream and he speaks with them and gives them answers. Then if someone asks, you can answer, "This person is saying the truth, that he saw the Prophet ﷺ and spoke to him."

And who in Islam among scholars and throughout the Muslim community did they say his book is the most accurate of all *ḥadīth* books? It is the book of Imam Bukhari ؓ. Imam Bukhari never wrote one *ḥadīth* that he heard from someone reliable without asking the Prophet ﷺ in a dream, and if the Prophet ﷺ authenticated it, saying it is correct, then Imam Bukhari wrote it, and this is known by all scholars. Even when he wanted to put a *ḥadīth* under a chapter, the Prophet ﷺ instructed him in a dream, saying, "Put this *ḥadīth* under this chapter or that chapter in your book." Imam Bukhari ؓ came more than three-hundred years after the time of Prophet ﷺ. He collected the *ḥadīth* and asked the Prophet ﷺ, "Did you say it, or you didn't say it?" and the Prophet ﷺ said, "Yes, I said it."

If Imam Bukhari, a non-Arab from Central Asia, was able to collect these *aḥadīth* and authenticate them from the Prophet ﷺ, what do you think of *awliyāullāh* who see the Prophet ﷺ in a dream and the Prophet ﷺ says to them, "Yes, I said that," or, "Yes, it is true and who recites that will get this reward." Do we say they are lying? No, and not even a normal person can lie and say, "I saw the Prophet ﷺ in a dream," because he fears the Prophet ﷺ. You cannot lie about that, although you might lie about everything else.

A well-known *ḥadīth* of the Prophet ﷺ states:

They asked the Prophet ﷺ, "Does a mu'min steal?" Prophet ﷺ replied, "Yes." Then they asked, "Does a mu'min commit adultery?" "Yes, that might be," said the Prophet ﷺ. Then they asked, "And does a mu'min lie?" He said, "No, a mu'min cannot lie."

So if you cannot lie to each other, how can you lie about the Prophet ﷺ? There are many *aḥadīth* that people read or hear that were confirmed by the Prophet ﷺ, such as the *ḥadīth* of Sayyīdinā Muhiyuddīn Ibn ʿArabi ق, one of the greatest saints, in his *Tafsīr Sūrat al-ʿAsr*:

وَالْعَصْرِ إِنَّ الْإِنسَانَ لَفِي خُسْرٍ إِلَّا الَّذِينَ آمَنُوا وَعَمِلُوا الصَّالِحَاتِ وَتَوَاصَوْا بِالْحَقِّ وَتَوَاصَوْا بِالصَّبْرِ

Wa 'l-ʿasr inna 'l-insāna la-fī khusr, illa 'Llādhīna āmanū wa ʿamilū 's-sālihati wa tawāsaw bi 'l-haqqa wa tawāsaw bi 's-sabir.

By al-'Asr (the time)! Verily, Mankind is in loss, except for those who have believed and done righteous deeds and exhorted each other to truth and exhorted each other to patience. (Sūrat al-ʿAsr, 103:1-3)

"*ʿAsr*" is the *ʿAsr* prayer and Allāh ﷻ is making an oath by it. It has various other meanings, such as "one century," "the time," and "the century that is sixty-three years of the life of the Prophet ﷺ." *Awlīyāullāh* say that in this *sūrah*, Allāh ﷻ is making this oath on the Prophet's ﷺ life. "I am giving an oath that human beings are losers, except those who believe and do good and advise each other toward goodness and prohibit what is bad." We are not going to give the *tafsīr* of *Sūrat al-ʿAsr* now because we already gave it ten years ago, you can find it; perhaps it filled ten CD's.

So Sayyīdinā Muhiyuddīn ق saw the Prophet ﷺ in a dream and asked him about this. Can we say he is lying? No, even a normal person cannot lie about whether or not he saw the Prophet ﷺ. Prophet ﷺ said, "Yes, I said that." What *ḥadīth* supports this?

The Prophet ﷺ said:

In saluhat ummatī falahā maʿayshata yawm wa in fasudat lahā maʿayashat nisfa yawm.

If my ummah is good Allāh will give the ummah the age of one day, and if it is corrupted Allāh will give it the age of half a day.[1] (Ibn ʿArabi)

وَإِنَّ يَوْمًا عِندَ رَبِّكَ كَأَلْفِ سَنَةٍ مِّمَّا تَعُدُّونَ

Wa inna yawma ʿinda rabbika ka-alfi sannatin mimma taʿudūn.

Verily a Day in the sight of thy Lord is like a thousand years of your reckoning. (Sūrat al-*Hajj*, 22:47)

So it means that Allāh gave the *ummah* a day-and-a-half of life, which is equal to 1,000 years of heavenly progress and the other 500 years (half a day) for when it will be corrupted. Look at how a thousand years ago Islam was booming with writers and scholars; everyone was writing about Islam and nothing else. Now Islamic knowledge is not being studied and it is going down. He said, "Yes, this *ummah* has fifteen-hundred years." We are now currently in 1433 Hijri. So seventy years remain for *ʿalamāt as-sughrā wa ʿalamāt al-kubrā,* all the small and big Signs of the Last Day to appear.

Ṣalawāt on the Prophet ﷺ is the theme of our discussion in the weeks that I am here, and when I travel I will mention these and they will be recorded, *inshā'Allāh.* There are so many benefits of making *ṣalawāt* on Sayyīdinā Muḥammad ﷺ. If Allāh ﷻ and His angels are praising Sayyīdinā Muḥammad ﷺ, what kind of benefits will you get if you praise him?

Yesterday we explained about Sayyīdinā Aḥmad al-Badawi's ؓ *ṣalawāt,* when Muḥammad al-Talmaysani ؓ completed *Dalāʾil al-Khayrāt* 100,000 times and he saw the Prophet ﷺ in a dream, saying, "O Muḥammad al-Talmaysani! If you read the *Ṣalāt* of Aḥmad al-Badawi, it will be as if you have completed *Dalāʾil al-Khayrāt* 800,000 times!" We haven't yet mentioned the rewards of actually reading *Dalāʾil al-Khayrāt,* which are endless, and he read it 100,000 times!

---

[1] Al-Munawī cites it in *Fayd al-Qadeer,* from Shaykh Muhiyuddeen Ibn `Arabi.

The Prophet ﷺ said if he read this *ṣalawāt*, he would get 800,000 times the reward! Prophet ﷺ mentioned the prayer of Sayyīdinā Aḥmad al-Badawi, and it reads:

اَللّٰهُمَّ صَلِّ وَسَلِّمْ وَبَارِكْ عَلَى سَيِّدِنَا وَمَوْلَانَا مُحَمَّدٍ شَجَرَةِ الأَصْلِ النُّورَانِيَّةِ، وَلَمْعَةِ القَبْضَةِ الرَّحْمَانِيَّةِ، وَأَفْضَلِ الخَلِيْقَةِ الإنْسَانِيَّةِ، وَأَشْرَفِ الصُّوْرَةِ الجِسْمَانِيَّةِ، وَمَعْدِنِ الأَسْرَارِ الرَّبَّانِيَّةِ، وَخَزَائِنِ العُلُوْمِ الاِصْطِفَائِيَّةِ، صَاحِبِ القَبْضَةِ الأَصْلِيَّةِ، وَالبَهْجَةِ السَّنِيَّةِ، وَالرُّتْبَةِ العَلِيَّةِ، مَن انْدَرَجَتِ النَّبِيُّوْنَ تَحْتَ لِوَائِهِ، فَهُمْ مِنْهُ وَإِلَيْهِ، وَصَلِّ وَسَلِّمْ وَبَارِكْ عَلَيْهِ وَعَلَى آلِهِ وَصَحْبِهِ عَدَدَ مَاخَلَقْتَ، وَرَزَقْتَ وَأَمَتَّ وَأَحْيَيْتَ إِلَى يَوْمِ تَبْعَثُ مَنْ أَفْنَيْتَ، وَسَلِّمْ تَسْلِيْمًاكَثِيْرًا وَالحَمْدُ لِلّٰهِ رَبِّ العَالَمِيْنَ

Allāhumma salli wa sallim wa bārik ʿala Sayyīdinā wa Mawlana Muḥammadin shajarati 'l-asli 'n-nūrāniyyati wa lamʿatil qabdati 'r-raḥmāniyyati wa afdali 'l-khalīqati 'l-insāniyyati wa ashrafi 's-sūrati 'l-jismāniyyati wa mʿadini 'l-asrāri 'r-rabBanīyyati wa khazāini 'l-ʿulūmi 'l-istifāiyyati, sāḥibi 'l-qabdati 'l-asliyya wa 'l-bahjati 's-saniyya wa 'r-rutbati 'l-ʿaliyya, man indarajati 'n-nabiyyūna tahta liwā'ihi, fahum minhu wa ilayhi, wa salli wa sallim wa bārik ʿalayhi wa ʿala ālihi wa sāḥbihi ʿadada mā khalaqta wa razaqta wa amatta wa ahyayta ilā yawmi tabʿathu man afnayta wa sallim taslīman kathīra wa 'l-hamdulillāhi rabbi 'l-ʿalamīn.

O Allāh! Bless, greet and sanctify our master and liege lord Muḥammad, the Tree of Original Light, the Sparkle of the Handful of Divine Mercy, the Best of All Humankind, the Noblest of Physical Frames, the Vessel of the Lord's Secrets and Storehouse of the Sciences of the Elect, the Possessor of the Original Divine Grasp, Resplendent Grace, and Uppermost Rank, under whose flag line up all the prophets, so that they are from him and point to him. Bless, greet and sanctify him and his Family and Companions, to the number of all that You have ever created, sustained, caused to die, and caused to live again, to the Day You resurrect those You reduced to dust, and greet him with an abundant and endless greeting. Glory and praise belong to Allāh, the Lord of the Worlds!

Fātiḥah.

Your duty is to print twenty to thirty copies of this *duʿa* and distribute it to people so they can read it and get that *barakah*. I am bringing these from authentic books in order to learn what our predecessors brought. It is not only to learn *shatahāt*, metaphorical (meanings) or something that no one can understand; we need something that gives us rewards and benefits as our predecessors received. Now, since there is so much darkness on Earth, when you read it you will receive even more than what they did.

About two-hundred years ago in Mecca al-Mukarrama, Shaykh ul-Islam of the Shafi'i school of thought, Aḥmad ibn Zayni Dahlan ؒ, said that one of the greatest *walis*, Abu al-Mawahib ash-Shadhili ق, said, "I saw the Prophet ﷺ in a dream and told him, '*Yā Rasūlullāh*! Allāh will pray ten times on whoever prays on you one time, isn't this so?"

That is *ḥadīth* of the Prophet ﷺ:

Man salla 'alayya marrah, sallallāhu 'alayhi 'ashara marrah.
Whoever prays on me one time, Allāh prays on him ten times. (Saḥiḥ)

Imam ash-Shadhili ق continued, "For the one who prays on you one time, does his heart need to be present or may it be absent? Many people recite *ṣalawāt* and at the same time converse with people and the heart is not present but the tongue is making *ṣalawāt*, so is that acceptable, or must your heart also be present?" The Prophet ﷺ said, "*Fa qāla lā*, it is not necessary. Even someone whose heart is *ghāfil*, heedless, and not present with me, if he prays on me one time Allāh ﷻ will give him mountains of angels." This means there are an infinite number of angels who will pray for him and ask forgiveness on his behalf. That is for someone who says, "*Allāhumma salli 'ala Sayyīdinā Muḥammad ﷺ wa 'ala ālihi wa sāḥbihi wa sallim*," and his heart is not with it, but with the people!

In the dream the Prophet ﷺ continued, "If his heart is present, no one knows what will be given to him except for Allāh ﷻ." That means the reward for one such *ṣalawāt* on the Prophet ﷺ is beyond any imagination or description! The question in the dream was whether the heart is present or the heart is heedless: if the heart is heedless, Allāh will give the likeness of mountains of angels praying and asking forgiveness on your behalf, and when someone is reaching to make this connection in their heart, then no one knows what Allāh will give!

It has been collected from the sayings of *awlīyāullāh* and *'arifīn* from a long time ago that if someone missed a lot of prayers and fasting, then they have to increase prayers on the Prophet ﷺ as much as possible. Why? Because whoever makes one prayer on the Prophet ﷺ, Allāh will make ten prayers for him. If you do one prayer, Allāh sends ten prayers for you, and each prayer will completely load the Scale and whatever sins you committed will be wiped out, and the Balance will be heavier on the side of *ṣalawāt*. Because you are doing prayers on the Prophet ﷺ according to your capacity, Allāh ﷻ is answering you according to His Greatness, and His Greatness describes His Lordship, which has no limits! So when He gives you rewards of ten prayers for each *ṣalāt,* those prayers of Allāh will overcome all that you missed of prayers and fasting and worship. That is *Ṭarīqat as-Ṣalāf,* the Way of the Predecessors; they encouraged their students to increase *ṣalawāt* on the Prophet ﷺ as it will save them from Hellfire and increase their love of the Prophet ﷺ and love of their shaykh who is guiding them through this tunnel.

It is more valuable to speak to students about these things than the state of trance that this one or that one is in. If I describe this water but don't give it to you, how will you know the *ladhdhāt,* pleasure of tasting it? So with *Ṣalāt ʿala an-Nabī* ﷺ you will reach to see this Light of Sayyida Rabiʿah al-ʿAdawiyya that we previously discussed; she saw the Light of the Prophet ﷺ and when her husband saw it he couldn't carry it and died.

If I say, "This is pure, tasty crystal water but I am not giving it to you to taste," and you just ate something spicy, so you could really do with this water, what would you do? Now I am one-hundred percent sure that people will go home after this and begin to make much *ṣalawāt* on the Prophet ﷺ, and will begin to slow down in one week! But *awlīyāullāh* said, *ajall al-karamāt dawām at-tawfiq,* "The best of miracles is to be consistent." You have to be consistent in what you are doing no matter how small, and do not drop it. The rewards of prayers on the Prophet ﷺ are so much that it has been mentioned in hundreds of *aḥadīth* in different ways to fit everyone's different needs. Some people like organic milk, others prefer lactose-free milk, and some like two-percent or non-fat milk. Everyone gets according to his capacity of handling the light of these prayers and whatever he likes to recite will be thrown in his heart.

That is why the Prophet ﷺ came with so many *ṣalawāt* that the *Saḥābah* ؓ recited. The best *faʿida,* benefit you get is by praising the Prophet ﷺ and we are going to go through all these benefits.

One is that you obeyed Allāh, when He said, "Obey Allāh, obey the Prophet, and obey those in authority among you." (4:59) Also, to obey Prophet ﷺ is Allāh's Order:

مَّنْ يُطِعِ الرَّسُولَ فَقَدْ أَطَاعَ اللَّهَ

Man yutī' 'ir-rasūl faqad 'ata Allāh.

Who obeys Prophet obeys Allāh. (Sūrat an-Nisa', 4:30)

Allāh ﷻ is saying, "O *Mu'mins*! Make *ṣalawāt* on Prophet!"

إِنَّ اللَّهَ وَمَلَائِكَتَهُ يُصَلُّونَ عَلَى النَّبِيِّ يَا أَيُّهَا الَّذِينَ آمَنُوا صَلُّوا عَلَيْهِ وَسَلِّمُوا تَسْلِيمًا

Inna-Llāha wa malā'ikatahu yusallūna 'ala 'n-nabiyy, yā ayyuhal-ladhīna āmanū sallū 'alayhi was sallimū taslīma.

Verily, Allāh and His angels send praise on the Prophet. O Believers! Pray upon him and greet him. (Sūrat al-'Aḥzāb, 33:56)

The Unimaginable Benefits of Salawat

1. **You are showing obedience to Allāh ﷻ and when you do that you will be saved in *dunya* and in *Akhirah*.** Don't say there is a question mark. Make sure to say, "There is no question mark! I'm going to go to Paradise because I'm praising Prophet ﷺ and that is my ticket to Paradise!" If you keep that belief in your heart, Allāh ﷻ will not let you down because He said, "Make *ṣalawāt* on Prophet," so do it! It may be a hundred times a day or even just once a day.

   Praising the Prophet ﷺ is considered *Al-'Ubūdiyya al-Mahdah*, the Pure Worship, because you are obeying Allāh ﷻ and at the same time obeying the Prophet ﷺ. So do that and be happy. Sing as much as you like! This was the first point, by which you will be considered a worshipper and will be forgiven for obeying Allāh ﷻ by making *ṣalawāt*!

2. **After you have done that, Allāh ﷻ will order angels to send *ṣalawāt* on you.** You will be dressed with angelic dresses from all kinds of angels that Allāh ﷻ created, all of whom will reward you with heavenly medallions, and only Allāh alone knows what He will give you! There are angels who praise standing and angels who praise bowing. Those standing are always standing; they cannot sit! They are standing all their lives and Allāh ﷻ will give them Eternal Life, as there

is eternal Paradise for *mu'mins* and for *mu'min jinn*. Those angels have been created standing and their eyes are on the one whom they are praising, Prophet ﷺ, and the *barakah* of their praises reflect on you when you are praising him!

As we said, the Prophet ﷺ is a mirror. Allāh and His angels are sending *ṣalawāt* on him and whatever *ṣalawāt* they are reciting, their eyes are constantly on him, praising him directly in his presence, not just hundreds and thousands of angels, but infinite numbers of angels! So when you pray once on the Prophet ﷺ, an infinite number of reflections of the angelic praisings on him come to you. What do you want better than that? These are the prayers of angels, who are *maʿsūm,* infallible, so they will dress us with these prayers!

There are some angels standing with no movement, some who are always bowing, and some who never raise their heads from *sajda*. There are also some angels who are sitting and some lying down. Allāh ﷻ knows best; we don't know.

"You will get ten *ṣalawāt* in return," means you will get ten times the amount of whatever they are praying on the Prophet ﷺ and the whole reflection of all those infinite number of angels praying on him will go to him and then be reflected on you! Imagine an infinite number of angels in every moment sending different types of *ṣalawāt* on Prophet ﷺ, all of which will be reflected on you! That is why in seclusion they tell you to recite at least 24,000 *ṣalawāt* a day to cover all these different appearances coming from Prophet's side to you. Although you might not see them, you still receive them.

3. **For every *salawāt* you recite, it is as if you have freed one slave.** Back then slavery was commonplace, so when you did *ṣalawāt* it was as if you had freed ten necks from slavery, but as there is no slavery now, it will be as if you have freed ten people from Hellfire!

There is one *ṣalawāt* all of you read and it will count as if you have read on the entire number of human beings, as if all human beings on Earth have made *ṣalawāt*! Grandshaykh ق said that *ṣalawāt* is what Great-Grandshaykh Sharafuddin ad-Daghestani ق recited. If you are in the presence of the Prophet ﷺ reciting that *ṣalawāt,* it is equal to all human beings from the time of Sayyīdinā Adam ﷺ to Judgment Day, making *ṣalawāt* in the presence of the Prophet ﷺ! That is the Sayyid as-*Ṣalawāt* of Grandshaykh ʿAbdAllāh ق:

ʿAlā ashrafi l-ʿalamīna Sayyīdinā Muḥammadini 's-ṣalawāt.

ʿAlā afdali l-ʿalamīna Sayyīdinā Muḥammadini 's-ṣalawāt.

ʿAlā akmali l-ʿalamīna Sayyīdinā Muḥammadini 's-ṣalawāt.

Salawātullāhi taʿala wa malā'ikatihi wa anbiyā'ihi wa rusūlihi wa jamīʿ khalqihi ʿalā Muḥammadin wa ʿalā āli Muḥammad, ʿalayhi wa ʿalayhimu 's-salām wa raḥmatullāhi taʿala wa barakātuh, wa radiyallāhu tabaraka wa taʿala ʿan sādātina as-ḥābi Rasūlillāhi ajmaʿīn, wa ʿani 't-tabiʿīna bihim bi-ihsān, wa ʿani l-'a'imati l-mujtahidīni 'l-mādin, wa ʿani l-ʿulamā'i 'l-muttaqqin, wa ʿani 'l-awliyāi 's-sālihīn, wa ʿam-mashayikhina fi 't-tarīqati n-Naqshbandiyyati l-ʿAlīyya, qaddas Allāhu taʿala arwāhahumu 'z-zakiyya, wa nawwarallāhu taʿala adrihatahumu 'l-mubaraka, wa aʿadallāhu taʿala ʿalayna min barakātihim wa fuyudātihim dā'iman wa 'l-hamdulillāhi Rabbi 'l-ʿalamīn.

This *ṣalawāt* is one whose rewards the angels are unable to write, as it is written by Allāh ﷻ Himself!

Prophetic Teachings of the 360 Points in Humans

I would like to mention one more thing, to say that we are not Buddhists or New Age people, but we are *Ahlu 'sh*-Shariʿah, the People of Islamic Shariʿah! Throughout Islamic History, regarding the Shariʿah, you see most of the great scholars are People of *Tasawwuf.* It is a fact; no one can argue this as we have a lot of evidence from big scholars. We are not interested in *taqlīd,* imitating Buddhists, with their hands like this or that (closing fingers and thumbs).

People are discussing and arguing about "(energy) points" or "no points" because they believe in points, is it not? Here you have (a *murīd*) who believed in *chakras* and points here and there, then there are also people who say there are no points. Even if Buddhists have points, we don't follow them, we follow the points that the Prophet ﷺ mentioned! The one who says there are no points is not educated, or he is not up to the standard to look at whether the Prophet ﷺ mentioned points or not! We follow what the Prophet ﷺ mentioned about points, not what Buddhists follow. It could be that Buddhists are taking from Muslims.

To say there are no points is to be uneducated, ignorant or illiterate, or you are "petting" some people to go along with them. And the evidence is in the *ḥadīth* of the Prophet ﷺ. There are many *aḥadīth* on that issue, but I will mention the *ḥadīth* of Imam Muslim. I will read it completely in order for those who understand Arabic to know there are points. That is why an acupuncturist inserts needles in these points, and if someone's back or leg hurts they go to a physical therapist. Pain management physicians, physical therapists and acupuncturists press or manipulate these points and it relieves the pain.

Islamic knowledge teaches us about these points in Prophetic Medicine. Everything in your life begins with a point. Even if you want to write, you begin with a point; at the beginning of writing there is a point and every letter consists of points that are connected with each other to describe that letter.

The Prophet ﷺ said:

Every one of the children of Adam has been created with 360 joints; so he who declares the Glory of Allāh, praises Allāh, declares Allāh to be One, Glorifies Allāh, and seeks forgiveness from Allāh, and removes an obstacle from people's path (like we have many obstacles in Cyprus blocking everyone), and enjoins what is good and forbids from evil, to the number of those three hundred and sixty joints or points, will walk that Day toward Paradise, having removed himself from Hell.

Every human being has 360 *mafsal*, points. You can keep them strong by reciting *takbīr, tahlīl, tahmīd* and *istighfār,* which is the way Muslims use points. If they know where the points are and press on them, saying, *"Allāhu Akbar,"* or *"Alḥamdulillāh,"* or *"SubḥānAllāh,"* or *"Astaghfirullāh,"* praising Allāh on these points, the body will be relieved and sickness will be taken away. It will be as if you paid *ṣadaqah* for the day and freed yourself from Hellfire.

In Imam Aḥmad's ؓ *Musnad,* he relates the same *ḥadīth* that says there are 360 points or joints in the body, and for each point there is a *ṣadaqah*:

I heard the Prophet say, "There are 360 joints (points) in the human body and for each joint you must give a ṣadaqah (thanks or charity) every day.

(Bukhari)

So every day you have to pay 360 *ṣadaqah* for every point. You can give one penny for each point, which will make $3.60, and giving this every day will relieve you from illnesses. I will continue on this perhaps from Cyprus. So based on the *ḥadīth* of the Prophet ﷺ, Muslims believe in 360 points, and if you press on them your body will move straight-forward, but if you don't press them your body won't. If you understand, you understand, and if not (O ignorant debaters) you are a donkey, as donkeys don't understand. If it makes you happy, so be it.

Egypt brought us some intelligent people who are Muslim doctors and who, at the same time, are studying *aḥadīth* of the Prophet ﷺ. They said, "We want to confirm this *ḥadīth* and check human beings to see if there are 360 points." Dr. Shareef Aḥmad Jalal, Dr. Aḥmad bin Mulhim, Dr. Mustafa Muḥammad ʿAbdul Mulhim, and Dr. Khalil Ibrahim Mullāh Khatir examined this issue and found proof and this is it, their findings! We aren't Buddhists because we say we believe in points, because Islam accepts and believes in points. We are Muslims, and we don't follow Buddhists, we follow our Prophet ﷺ! Don't deny this out of ignorance, laughing and saying there are no points, as there are points! These medical doctors along with a doctor of Sharʿiah studied this and found it to be true.

I will read examples of some of the points they identified: 76 vertebral column, pelvis; 2 atlanto-occipital; 69 lumbosacral; 3 shoulder; 1 sacro-coccygea; 1 symphysis pubis; 86 skull; 6 throat; 66 chest. [2]

On the last page, in Arabic it says, "*Mafasil al-Jumjumah,* the Points in the Skull." Everyone has a stubborn head and thinks he is above everyone, so he doesn't respect other's viewpoint without evidence and, therefore, we are giving evidence. The skull has 86 joints or points, 80 of which you can press and fix the body. Do you (who said there are no points) know that, before you say there are no points? There are prophetic points! The points of hunjara in the throat are six, the points on the chest are 66, and these are different from the seven *latā'if,* areas of energy on the chest that *awlīyāullāh* accept, and the one rejecting that knows there are seven *latā'if.*

---

[2] For full list, go to http://www.twitlonger.com/show/gk2o61

Mafasil al-Atraf al-'Ulwiyya, The Points of the Upper Body, are 64; the joints of the lower body are 62, and in total there are 360. The Prophet ﷺ mentioned 1400 years ago that there are 360 points in the body and if you press on them you will recover. For this you need someone who is an expert in Prophetic Medicine and who is a wali. This appeared to us like a perfect moon of the significant miracles of the Holy Qur'an and the prophetic, pure *sunnah*! No one would know that in the time of the Companions ؓ, because Allāh ﷻ said:

سَنُرِيهِمْ آيَاتِنَا فِي الْآفَاقِ وَفِي أَنفُسِهِمْ

Sanurīhim āyatina fi 'l-afāqi wa fi anfusihim hatta yatabayyana lahum annahu 'l-haqq.

We will show them Our signs in all the horizons and in themselves, until it is clear to them that it is the truth. (Sūrat al-Fussilat, 41:53)

That keeps the reality of *wa fi anfusihim hatta yatabayyana lahum annah ul-haqq*, "In the future we will show them scientific signs to show them that Holy Qur'an is true and the Holy Prophet is true." So these are the points we follow according to the *ḥadīth* of the Prophet ﷺ.

We will mention more on that in the next session, *inshā'Allāh*. You coming here is not for nothing, it is to get these treasures!

Allāh ﷻ said in Holy Qur'an:

يَا أَيُّهَا النَّاسُ اتَّقُوا رَبَّكُمُ الَّذِي خَلَقَكُم مِّن نَّفْسٍ وَاحِدَةٍ وَخَلَقَ مِنْهَا زَوْجَهَا وَبَثَّ مِنْهُمَا رِجَالًا كَثِيرًا وَنِسَاءً وَاتَّقُوا اللَّهَ الَّذِي تَسَاءَلُونَ بِهِ وَالْأَرْحَامَ إِنَّ اللَّهَ كَانَ عَلَيْكُمْ رَقِيبًا

Yā ayyuha 'n-nasu 't-taqū rabbakumu 'l-ladhī khalaqakum min nafsin wahidatin wa khalaqa minha zawjaha wabaththa minhuma rijālan kathīran wa nisā-an wattaqu-Llāhalladhī tasā-alūna bihi wa 'l-arhama inna-Llāha kana 'alaykum raqīb.

O Mankind! Fear your Lord, Who created you from one soul and created from it its mate and dispersed from both of them many men and women.

(Sūrat an-Nisā', 4:1)

Evolutionists say that everything came from one cell and Allāh ﷻ mentioned in the Holy Qur'an that He created all of humanity from one soul, and from that soul its companion, and from them Allāh ﷻ brought up many men and women. From one cell, one soul! Allāh ﷻ ordered Jibrīl ﵇ to go to Earth and with one hand scoop some earth (soil), meaning one point. He took it to Paradise and from this Allāh ﷻ created Sayyīdinā Adam ﵇. It means, "begin with one." Allāh ﷻ began with one point: we were one cell from one sperm that swam among 200 million sperm and it hit one egg. Out of 200 million, Allāh ﷻ picks only one, one point.

Everything begins from one point and a sperm is even smaller than a point; if you put a point from a pen on paper you can see it, but you cannot see the sperm (it is not visible to the eye), and the egg is also hidden (within the womb). You can see the sperm when it comes out, but you never see the egg. That means Allāh ﷻ honored women not to be seen! He covered them, because they are so honorable and noble. He is hiding the egg and its realities in the womb of the mother with His Cover, but you can see the sperm (as it leaves the body). In any case, it is one point; everything begins with one and from that one, Allāh ﷻ created Creation. He ﷻ said, *alladhī khalaqakum min nafsin wahidah,* "(The One) Who created you from one soul." (4:1) Allāh ﷻ said to the Prophet ﷺ:

ثُمَّ دَنَا فَتَدَلَّى فَكَانَ قَابَ قَوْسَيْنِ أَوْ أَدْنَى

Fakana Qāba Qawsayni aw Adnā.

And he was at a distance of two bow lengths or nearer.

(Sūrat an-Najm, 53:8-9)

Qāba Qawsayni aw Adnā, "Two bows' length or less." "*Adnā*" means "less," which can be a point. That is why too many people spoke about points, not knowing about Prophetic Medicine. Today the Chinese use those points to heal. If you deny that, why do you go to a physical therapist? If you say there is no Prophetic Medicine, don't go to the doctor or a physical therapist! If you want to say there is no education in medicine, why do you immediately run to the doctor when someone gets sick?

Surrender to Allāh! You are surrendering to the doctor, not to Allāh ﷻ. And then you speak about high levels and how we will reach *Qāba Qawsayni aw Adnā* and how far we are from there. No, let us speak on something that we can reach, not something too high that we cannot reach.

May Allāh ﷻ forgive us and may Allāh ﷻ bless us.

Wa min Allāhi 't-tawfiq, bi ḥurmati 'l-ḥabīb, bi ḥurmati 'l-Fātiḥah.

And with Allāh is success. For the sake of the Beloved, for his sake we recite the opening chapter of Holy Qur'an.

Who Will See the Prophet in this Life

A'ūdhu billāhi min ash-Shayṭāni 'r-rajīm. Bismillāhi' r-Raḥmāni 'r-Raḥīm.
Nawaytu 'l-arbā'īn, nawaytu 'l-'itikāf, nawaytu'l-khalwah, nawaytu 'l-'uzlah,
nawaytu 'r-riyāḍa, nawaytu 's-sulūk, lillāhi Ta'alā fī hādhā 'l-masjid.
Atī'ūllāha wa atī'ū 'r-Rasūla wa ūlī 'l-amri minkum.
Obey Allāh, obey the Prophet, and obey those in authority among you. (4:59)

Dastūr, madad yā Sulṭān al-Awlīyā, Mawlana Shaykh Nazim al-Haqqani ق.
Dastūr, madad yā Sulṭān al-Awlīyā, Mawlana Shaykh 'AbdAllāh ad-Daghestani ق.

We ask Allāh ﷻ for the sake of the Prophet ﷺ to give our teacher, Sulṭān al-Awlīyā Mawlana Shaykh Nazim al-Haqqani, a healthy and long life to see Sayyīdinā Mahdi ؏ and for all of us to be healthy and to be with Mawlana Shaykh and to see Mahdi ؏. We ask for anyone, any *mu'min*, Muslim or even any non-believer to see Mahdi ؏ and that the Muslim or *mu'min* is brought higher and higher and that the non-believer will come back to his original and complete religion, about which Allāh ﷻ said:

أَنَّ الدِّينَ عِندَ اللهِ الإِسْلاَمُ

Inna ad-dīna 'inda Allāhi al-islām.
The religion in Allāh's view is Islam (submission to His Will).
(Sūrat Āli-'Imrān, 3:19)

The Prophet ﷺ brought what was revealed to him. He ﷺ said, "I was a prophet when Sayyīdinā Adam ؏ was between water and clay" (and in other *ḥadīths*, "between soul and body.").

Let's review the *ṣalawāt* of Aḥmad al-Badawi ؄ because it is good to memorize it and recite it. It is mentioned by *awlīyāullāh*, because they get inspiration from the Prophet ﷺ. When *awlīyāullāh* are in complete meditation through their soul and spirit, they have power to see what cannot be seen, hear what cannot be heard, as in the famous *Ḥadīth Qudsī* in which Allāh ﷻ spoke to Prophet ﷺ:

Wa lā yazāla ʿabdī yataqarabu ilayya bi 'n-nawāfil hatta uhibbah. Fa idhā ahbābtahu kuntu samaʿuhulladhī yasmaʿu bihi wa basarahulladhī yubsiru bihi, wa yadahulladhī yabtishu bihā wa rijlahullatī yamshī bihā.

My servant does not cease to approach Me through voluntary worship until I will love him. When I love him, I will become the ears with which he hears, the eyes with which he sees, the hand with which he acts, and the legs with which he walks (and other versions include, "and the tongue with which he speaks.").

(*Ḥadīth Qudsī*, Bukhari)

The Islamic heritage is that after the time of the Prophet ﷺ, through the time of the *Saḥābah* ❁ and all the *awlīyāullāh* until today, there were so many visions through dreams. These visions or dreams are a kind of inspiration or association through spirits with the Prophet ﷺ and no one can deny that. Many people around the world today have these experiences, so don't say it only happened before when people were more pious and less sinful, and today they are more sinful and less pious, and still people see the Prophet ﷺ in dreams, is it not? I am asking this small crowd here, how many of you saw the Prophet ﷺ in a dream? (*Some raise their hands.*)

The Prophet ﷺ said:

Man ra'ānī fir-ru'ya fa sa-yarānī haqqan.

Whoever saw me in a dream will see me in reality.

The Prophet ﷺ said, "Shayṭan and *jinn* can come in any form, but cannot come in the form of the Prophet ﷺ." So when you see the Prophet ﷺ that is a true reality, even if you see the hair of the Prophet ﷺ in a dream, not even in reality. In reality, many of you have seen the holy hair of the Prophet ﷺ, and if you see just the holy hair of the Prophet ﷺ you have seen the Prophet ﷺ, because Shayṭan cannot come in the shape of a hair of the Prophet ﷺ, it is impossible!

Man ra'ānī fi 'l-manām fa sayarānī fi'l-yaqazha.

Whoever saw me in a dream will see me in reality.

Imam Suyuti ❁ said, "They will see him in *dunya*." Everyone on the Last Day will run after the Prophet ﷺ, but in *dunya* you will see him. What can prevent his appearance? For example, if you open the electrical switch the light comes on. If the Prophet ﷺ wants his Light to appear, can anyone stop it? They cannot.

Al-mu'min mirāta akhī.

The mu'min is the mirror of his brother.

To Recognize One's Blindness

If a *mu'min* is a mirror of his brother, what about Prophet ﷺ? A mirror reflects your light and when you stand in front of it you see yourself. The *ḥadīth* says that if you stand in front of a *mu'min*, whatever behavior you see in him is actually from you, because he is a mirror reflecting you; therefore, if you see bad character, that is your bad character, and if you see good character, then you are good. That is the *ḥadīth*, "The believer is the mirror of his brother."

So what do you think about the Prophet ﷺ? We cannot reach anyone except we are with, but the Prophet ﷺ can reach anyone at any time. There are 1.5 billion Muslims on Earth, and if anyone makes *ṣalawāt* on the Prophet ﷺ he is there with him. Can you mention him and he doesn't come and respond? No, he comes to you, but you just don't see him because your ego is there. We said the *mu'min* is a mirror, so what about the Prophet ﷺ? He is not a mirror, he is multiple mirrors! When you put mirrors in a certain way you see infinite mirrors and your image reflects in each one, so what about the Prophet ﷺ?

If you call, "*Yā Sayyidī! Yā Rasūlullāh!*" will he not change us from bad to good? Yes, we are bad, we commit sins, but this doesn't prevent us from increasing our request to the Prophet ﷺ to see him. We make *ṣalawāt* and we are not seeing the Prophet ﷺ, that is for sure. No one can lie and say, "We are seeing him." Is this true or not? Why is this? It's not because the Prophet ﷺ is not there when you are making *ṣalawāt*; he is there but he is a mirror, so when you do not see him, that is blocked from you and it means you are blind. Therefore, you have to know you are spiritually blind and then improve yourself.

People say, "We are doing all the *awrād*, not only reciting 1500 '*Allāh, Allāh,*' but 2500." Some are even reciting 25,000 *ṣalawāt*. When I was in seclusion and I was doing 24,000 *ṣalawāt*, which takes four hours if you are quick and if you are slow it takes eight hours. If you are blind you are blind, but that doesn't mean you are not getting a response from the Prophet ﷺ. No, for each *ṣalawāt* there is a response, but our character is earthly and his character is of *Qāba Qawsayni aw Adnā*, as he ﷺ said:

أدبني ربي فأحسن تأديبي

Adabanī rabbī fa'aḥsana tā'dībī.

My Lord perfected my good manners and conduct. (Ibn ʿAsakir)

This means not just discipline, but in Arabic it is more, meaning, "I received my discipline directly from the Perfect One, the Creator." Or we can use the words, "He perfected my character." Allāh ﷻ didn't say that about anyone except Prophet ﷺ, when He said, "I dressed his character from My Greatness."

In this case, *"fa'aḥsana"* has a deep meaning in Arabic; here it means not only "perfected," but perfected beyond what you can imagine, according to Allāh's Greatness. In Arabic we say something is *"ḥasan,"* good, and if we say something is *"aḥsan"* then it is more extremely good. The Prophet ﷺ is *aḥsana*, above 'good,' he is unlimited good!

Allāh made seven Heavens and seven Earths. We are on one Earth and in one Heaven, so where are the other six Earths? That *ayah* indicates there are Creations other than this Creation and Allāh mentioned them as "Earth," so it means there are Earths other than ours upon which Creations are living. Who is their prophet? Who went to *Qāba Qawsayni aw Adnā*? Was it any prophet other than Sayyīdinā Muḥammad ﷺ? All other prophets came on this Earth, but Allāh ﷻ appointed Sayyīdinā Muḥammad ﷺ to reach above Paradises, above Heavens, above the ʿArsh and above the Seven Earths, one of them on which we live. That means he is prophet to all of them!

Yā Sayyidī! We are helpless, we are sending our *ṣalawāt* and we are seeing nothing, so that indicates we are blind. How does this differ from *awlīyāullāh*? When a *wali* sends his *ṣalawāt*, they see appearances in which the Prophet ﷺ appears in different ways. So many appearances have happened in Islamic history to countless *awlīyā* who were able to see the Prophet ﷺ. Rabiʿa al-ʿAdawiyya saw such appearances. Why am I giving an example of Rabiʿa al-ʿAdawiyya? To say that high level is not only for men, but it is also for ladies. If ladies get it, for sure men get that if they were on this discipline and have love for the Prophet ﷺ

Muḥammad al-Busayri ؓ wrote in his *al-Burdah ash-Sharīfa, wa mablagh al-ʿilmi fīhi annahu basharun wa annahu khayru khalqillāh kullihimi,* "The limit of knowledge concerning him is that he is a human being and that he is the best of all of Allāh's Creation." He recited that *qasīda* at night, but not by writing and thinking; rather, he sat next to the Nile River and put his feet in the flowing water, reciting that over and over. Just then, a *wali* and 700 *murīds* approached the Nile on their way to Mecca. That night they slept by the river bank and they needed a shower in the morning, but they found the river water was boiling. Grandshaykh, may Allāh bless his soul, mentioned this story, like the story of Rabiʿah al-ʿAdawiyya.

They were not able to wash in the river, but all of them needed to pray *Fajr* and they could not. That *wali* was *Sulṭān al-Awlīyā* from the Naqshbandi Golden Chain in that time. In the morning they brought water for him, so he made *wudu* and said, "This water is very hot."

They said to him, "*Yā Sayyidī,* we all need to take a shower but the water is boiling, so we cannot."

He said, "Make *tayammum* and I will lead the prayer."

He made *wudu* and they prayed, then he said, "I will lead you up the river to find the reason." They walked up to the shore and found Muḥammad al-Busayri ؓ with his foot extended in the river and he was reciting. He was not reciting like when you make poetry *ex tempore,* but it was coming by itself from the beginning up to the point when he says, *wa mablaghu 'l-ʿilmi fīhi annahu basharun,* "The highest of knowledge is that he is a human being," and whatever people think, they think he is a human and *awlīyāullāh* are amazed. He kept reciting that, and he was stuck on, "*Wa mablaghu 'l-ʿilmi fīhi annahu basharun,*" and he was unable to continue the recitation, *Wa annahu khayru 'l-khalqi kullihimi,* "Verily he is the best of Allāh's Creation over all Creation."

The *Sulṭān al-Awlīyā* ق of that time was there with his *murīds* and he saw al-Busayri was stuck on that verse, then that *Sulṭān al-Awlīyā* saw the presence of Prophet ﷺ, who said, *Wa annahu khayru 'l-khalqi kullihimi,* "Verily he is the best of Allāh's Creation, over all Creation." That was inspired from the Prophet ﷺ and that was an appearance seen by that *wali,* the *Sulṭān al-*

Awlīyā, but not by the *murīds.* He saw the appearance of the Prophet ﷺ, who was continuing the verse, *"wa annahu khayru 'l-khalqi kullihim. "Khalq"* is anything created, not just human beings. He was stuck, saying, "He is a *bashar*, a human being," but the Prophet ﷺ continued and added, "Not only *bashar*, but he is better than any other Creation (among *jinn,* angels, nature, herbs, animals)."

That is why I mentioned the Seven Earths, which is something in *'ijāzu 'l-Qur'an.* We know there are six other Earths, but we don't know what Creations are there. We know there are Creations there and Sayyīdinā Muḥammad ﷺ is the prophet for them; Allāh ﷻ gave him that power to appear with no restriction. We know from *ḥadīth* of the Prophet ﷺ that if someone dies as a *mu'min* his soul is free; it is not restricted, he can go anywhere with his soul. You cannot see, but he can see. If someone is not a *mu'min* or Muslim, he will have problems. Not everyone reached the level of *Imān.* You are Muslim and you said, *"Lā ilāha illa-Llāh Muḥammadun Rasūlullāh,"* but to reach the level of Imān and for your soul to be completely free, that is only for some. *Awlīyāullāh* can reach their followers, even after they die. If they can reach them, then the Prophet ﷺ can reach anyone!

Rabi'ah al-'Adawiyya ق was blessed because of her patience with her husband; she was not "eating his ears (nagging)" I am speaking of a particular woman, Rabi'ah, but in general there are men who "eat the ears" of their wives and wives who "eat the ears" of their husbands! Rabi'ah al-'Adawiyya's husband came home drunk after midnight and still she offered him food or whatever he wanted, and she never complained.

Allāh ﷻ made rules to obey and if you follow with obedience you will reach the level where you see appearances of the Prophet ﷺ. She was in obedience to what the Prophet ﷺ ordered her to do in Shari'ah and she was not complaining. Shari'ah orders, "Don't complain," and this is for men or women! But people complain, saying, "My father/brother /husband did this...." Everyone complains, but she did not.

He would come home after midnight and slap her one, two, three times, who knows how many times, and she prepared the food and brought it to him. He would fall asleep, and she stayed until he was awake and then give him his food. When he was out of the house, she stayed in her room praying and making *ṣalawāt* on the Prophet ﷺ. We will explain later some of the benefit of *ṣalawāt* on the Prophet ﷺ.

One day she was in her room and although it was not the time for her husband to come, he came home. This was unusual, not the normal time that he usually came. She was in her room making *ṣalawāt* and *istighfār* and he saw this huge light coming from there. He felt it and then she felt him and she knew he was there. She came out and closed the door, but he insisted on coming in her room.

He said, "You were speaking to someone and I want to know who it is." The beauty of that Light coming from the door was putting him in a trance and he insisted.

She said, "No, I cannot open it for you." He insisted, but she said, "No, I cannot do that." He still insisted on going in, so she said, "No, just look through the keyhole."

He looked through the keyhole and fell down, dead! That was the Light of the Prophet ﷺ; he was unable to take that, but she was able to carry those appearances.

So for *awlīyāullāh,* there are always appearances from the Prophet ﷺ. That is why Imam Abu al-Ḥasan ash-Shadili ق wrote *Dalā'il al-Khayrāt*, and people read part of it with love and it changes their lives. *Awlīyāullāh* are instructed, just as Muḥammad al-Busayri ق was instructed to add that verse to *Burdah ash-Sharīfa,* and they are instructed in what they need to tell their followers. They also get these appearances to receive the *awrāds,* so don't think the *awrād* is coming from nowhere. It is why they say, "Read this 92 times, etc." These are numbers you cannot exceed or lower; you have to be accurate on their count.

Later you may want to recite more, and I give the example of when you see people today who are playing games on the computer. When they finish one stage, they go to another stage, is it not? It opens up more and more. In the same way, the *awrād* will open for you one stage after another stage, more and more, until you reach the stage where these appearances begin to come. There are some principles you must follow, and if we do this we will be able to see what people cannot see and hear what people cannot hear. So keep your *ṣalawāt* on the Prophet ﷺ and keep the *barakah* to dress you, then Allāh will give you more and more.

When *awlīyāullāh* enter seclusion, there are many ways to do it, but it cannot be observed in a place where there is trouble, such as in the Middle

East. Mawlana Shaykh Nazim, may Allāh give him long life, accepted his current sickness as seclusion; he didn't talk or eat. I was there when he said, "From what Allāh ﷻ and the Prophet ﷺ opened, I cannot express what is coming. Huge changes are going to occur everywhere."

We see that Syria is ending, and now Mali and other African nations have opened (to political conflict) and there may be more to follow as this will continue. This is a game, like when children play video games they finish the first stage and then it opens to the second, then the third, one after another. That is why the Prophet ﷺ mentioned that in the Last Days too much killing is going to happen on Earth. Who expected so much killing to go on around the Earth? This is a sign, "O human beings! Open your eyes, open your hearts, open your ears. Keep yourself connected to the Prophet ﷺ through your teacher, making *ṣalawāt* on him. That is our *safinat an-najāt,* the ship of safety." *Astaghfirullāh.*

May Allāh ﷻ forgive us and may Allāh ﷻ bless us.

Wa min Allāhi 't-tawfiq, bi ḥurmati 'l-ḥabīb, bi ḥurmati 'l-Fātiḥah.

And with Allāh is success. For the sake of the Beloved, for his sake we recite the opening chapter of Holy Qur'an.

Salawat that Immediately Raise You

A'ūdhu billāhi min ash-Shayṭāni 'r-rajīm. Bismillāhi' r-Raḥmāni 'r-Raḥīm.
Nawaytu 'l-arbā'īn, nawaytu 'l-'itikāf, nawaytu'l-khalwah, nawaytu 'l-'uzlah,
nawaytu 'r-riyāḍa, nawaytu 's-sulūk, lillāhi Ta'ālā fī hādhā 'l-masjid.
Atī'ūllāha wa atī'ū 'r-Rasūla wa ūlī 'l-amri minkum.
Obey Allāh, obey the Prophet, and obey those in authority among you. (4:59)

Dastūr, madad yā Sulṭān al-Awlīyā, Mawlana Shaykh Nazim al-Haqqani ق.
Dastūr, madad yā Sulṭān al-Awlīyā, Mawlana Shaykh 'AbdAllāh ad-Daghestani ق.

Alḥamdulillāh, we have spoken of the importance of ṣalawāt on the Prophet ﷺ in different ways. One of them originated from Sayyīdinā 'Alī ؑ, which is part of the ṣalawāt we recite every day. In his book "Nahj ul-Muttaqīn, Peak of the God-Fearing," Sayyīdinā 'Alī ؑ said, man salla 'alā an-Nabī ﷺ bi hāūlāi kalimāti fī kulli yawmin thalātha marrāt wa fī kulli 'l-jumu'ah miyata marratin..., "Whoever makes ṣalawāt on the Prophet ﷺ with these words three times every day and a hundred times on Jumu'ah day will benefit from them as if all of Creation, all Muslims on Earth, all mu'min jinn and all angels have made ṣalawāt on the Prophet ﷺ."

Different awlīyāullāh from around the world, like Imam Jazuli ق who compiled Dalā'il al-Khayrāt, have taught us. He was not a Naqshbandi, he was from the Shadili Ṭarīqah and is buried in Marrakech, Morocco, but his Dalā'il al-Khayrāt is being read all over the world by every Muslim seeking the presence of the Prophet ﷺ in his Gnostic journey! Grandshaykh 'AbdAllāh al-Fa'iz ad-Daghestani ق and Mawlana Shaykh Nazim ق, including all Imams after the time of Imam al-Jazuli ق, and all Naqshbandis are reading Dalā'il al-Khayrāt. They don't say, "Why should we read from Dalā'il al-Khayrāt when he isn't a Naqshbandi?" Awlīyāullāh have a relationship with each other; therefore, they take from one another and know how important Dalā'il al-Khayrāt is for the seeker.

The ṣalawāt Sayyīdinā 'Alī ؑ related is one way of making ṣalawāt, which is part of the recitations of the Naqshbandi Order, so it is not coming only from Sayyīdinā Abu Bakr as-Siddiq ؑ; perhaps the first part of the recitation is from Sayyīdinā Abu Bakr, but we cannot say Naqshbandis only take from him as they also take from the lineage of Sayyīdinā 'Alī ؇ through Sayyīdinā Ja'far as-Sadiq ؇, which is why we say we are taking from both sides.

Get the Reward of All Salawat Ever Recited

So if you recite the *ṣalawāt* Sayyīdinā 'Alī ؇ related three times a day and a hundred times on Fridays, you will get the reward of all that Allāh ؇ created, as everything makes *ṣalawāt* on the Prophet ؇! How many Muslims are there around the world and how many *ṣalawāt* do they recite each day? If you add them all up along with the *ṣalawāt* of all angels, *ṣalawāt al-khalq* and *ṣalawāt jami'ī al-khalq*, as Sayyīdinā 'Alī ؇ mentioned, gathering the *ṣalawāt* of all Creation including *mu'min jinn* and other Creations, it will be as if you made that number of *ṣalawāt* when you recite this three times a day. Sayyīdinā 'Alī ؇ said, *man salla 'ala an-nabi ؇*, "Whoever makes *ṣalawāt* on the Prophet ؇ in this way," which means you do *ṣalawāt* one way, he does it another way and that one does it some other way, and it will be as though you have made *ṣalawāt* on the Prophet ؇ in all these ways with all the angels!

Also, *ṣalawāt wa hushira yawm al-qiyamat ma' an-nabi ؇*, "You will be resurrected on the Day of Judgment with the prophets," as mentioned in the Holy Qur'an:

وَمَن يُطِعِ اللَّهَ وَالرَّسُولَ فَأُوْلَـٰئِكَ مَعَ الَّذِينَ أَنْعَمَ اللَّهُ عَلَيْهِم مِّنَ النَّبِيِّينَ وَالصِّدِّيقِينَ وَالشُّهَدَاءِ وَالصَّالِحِينَ وَحَسُنَ أُولَـٰئِكَ رَفِيقًا

Wa man yuti'i Allāha wa 'r-rasūla fa'ūlāika ma' 'Lladhīna an'am Allāhu 'alayhim min an-nabiyyīna wa 's-siddiqīna wa 'sh-shuhadā' wa 's-sālihīna wa hasuna ūlā'ika rafiqa.

All who obey Allāh and the Prophet are in the company of those on whom is the grace of Allāh, of the prophets (who teach), the sincere (lovers of Truth), the witnesses (who testify), and the righteous (who do good). Ah, what a beautiful fellowship! (Sūrat an-Nisa', 4:69)

Allāh ؇ is saying, *ma'alladhīna an'ama Allāhu 'alayhim min an-nabiyyīna wa 's-siddiqīna wa 'sh-shuhadā' wa 's-sālihīna*, "Be with the prophets, the veracious, the martyrs and the pious," and Prophet ؇ will take your hand until you enter his place in Paradise!

Now there is an astonishing question that makes one ask, "How can I possibly understand that? It is too big!" The question is, if I made this *ṣalawāt* along with ten other people, we will all be with the Prophet ﷺ, is it not? Then how is the Prophet ﷺ going to take the hands of ten people? You can take the hand of two people, but you can't take the hand of ten people! So how would he do that? Forget ten, as it is not only ten who are making *ṣalawāt*, but it is millions and millions! One time I heard Grandshaykh ق say, "Ummat an-*Nabī* ﷺ consists of four-hundred billion human beings, all of whom make *ṣalawāt* on the Prophet ﷺ!" So then how is the Prophet ﷺ going to take four-hundred billion hands at the same time? That is the greatness of the Prophet, ﷺ to whom Allāh ﷻ gave that secret from His Beautiful Names and Attributes to take the hand of everyone! He will be like a mirror that you look into and see hundreds of reflections! One of his many reflections or *rūhaniyyah,* realities, will accompany each person, taking each one with his level.

Allāh ﷻ said in the Holy Qur'an:

وَنَحْنُ أَقْرَبُ إِلَيْهِ مِنْ حَبْلِ الْوَرِيدِ

Wa nahnu aqrabu ilayhi min habli 'l-warīd.

And We are nearer to you than your jugular vein. (Sūrat al-Qāf, 50:16)

وإعلموا أن فيكم رسول الله

W'alamū anna fīkum rasūlullāh.

And know Allāh's Messenger is in you. (Sūrat al-Ḥujurāt, 49:7)

"The Prophet ﷺ is within you," not by himself, but by his holy manifestation. His reflection appears in you because Allāh ﷻ created human beings from three Lights: the Light of Allāh, Light of the Prophet ﷺ and the Light of Sayyīdinā Adam ﷺ. So that appearance of Light will come out of his greatness, and these spiritualites will appear in the form of his picture. Therefore, you feel yourself holding the hand of the Prophet ﷺ.

To every person a different *tajallī* appears and it may be as the shaykh or any other form that the Prophet ﷺ wants you to see. So *awlīyāullāh* have many different appearances of the Prophet ﷺ coming to them and they can be in the presence of the Prophet ﷺ at any time, but normal people may feel something when reciting, except they cannot see the presence of the Prophet

ﷺ as they are spiritually blind. *Awlīyāullāh* can see the Prophet ﷺ, as they say in Urdu, he is *hāzir,* "present," and *nāzir,* "sees." So he is waiting for you to make *ṣalawāt,* and we say, *"Allāhumma salli 'ala Sayyīdinā Muḥammad* ﷺ*!"*

That is why there are some groups of people that when name of the Prophet ﷺ comes they say, *"Allāhumma salli 'ala Muḥammad wa 'ala āli Muḥammad*!" We, Ahlu'l-*Sunnah* wa 'l-Jama'ah, don't open our mouth, and in the time of the Ottomans when the name of the Prophet ﷺ was mentioned, all of them stood up—the sultan, the queen, the princes and princesses, everyone!

We ask the Prophet ﷺ to look at us and to defeat our enemies; we ask your vision on us *yā Aba Zahra, yā Aba Zahra lillāhi nazhra, lā tukhayibna... "O father of Zahra! Gaze on us, don't let us down for the sake of Allāh, and we are your guests so don't refuse us!"* Will the Prophet ﷺ refuse anyone? There is no way! If you ask from your heart, he will answer. Say, *"Yā Sayyidī, yā Rasūlullāh lillāhi nazhra,* We are your guests, don't refuse us!" May Allāh ﷻ keep us with our shaykh, Mawlana Shaykh Nazim al-Haqqani ق!

The Dowry of Fatimah az-Zahra

When we call on Prophet ﷺ he answers and he is present, but we are blind and we don't see it. Just now that *tajallī* and appearance came with the *barakah* of Grandshaykh ق and Mawlana Shaykh Nazim ق for the sake of Sayyida Fatimah az-Zahra ؓ, when Prophet ﷺ said to her, "*Yā* Fatimah! I want you to marry and 'Alī ؓ is proposing to you."

She said, "No I don't want to." That was so great, that she refused Sayyīdinā 'Alī's proposal and the Prophet ﷺ was surprised.

Sayyīdinā Jibrīl ؑ came and said, "*Yā Rasūlullāh*! Ask her why."

And the Prophet ﷺ said, "*Yā* Fatimah! Why are you refusing your cousin, the first young one to come to Islam?"

She replied, "*Yā Rasūlullāh*! When you were born, you came out of your mother's womb saying, *ummatī, ummatī,* 'My nation, my nation,' and when throughout your life you are saying, 'My nation,' and when you are dying you are saying, 'My nation,' and in the grave you are saying, 'My nation,' and in *Akhirah* you are saying, 'My nation.' So if you want me to marry

Sayyīdinā 'Alī ؓ, my dowry must be your nation, the whole *ummah* of Sayyīdinā Muḥammad ﷺ."

Now if the Prophet ﷺ agrees and she marries him, it means on the Day of Judgment she wants the whole *ummah* to be with her, or else her marriage to Sayyīdinā 'Alī ؓ will not be correct.

Prophet ﷺ said, "I cannot answer."

Jibrīl ؑ came and said, "Allāh ﷻ is accepting that your dowry be the nation of Sayyīdinā Muḥammad ﷺ."

Grandshaykh ق said, "That appearance came to Fatimah az-Zahra ؓ and when the Prophet ﷺ will come to ask *shafa'ah* for the *ummah*, she will stand up and say, 'Give me my dowry,' then Allāh ﷻ will say to her, 'Take your dowry,' and she will go to Paradise with them!"

She did not live too long; when the Prophet ﷺ left *dunya*, she also left *dunya* shortly after as she was so near to Sayyīdinā Muḥammad ﷺ.

So Sayyīdinā 'Alī ؓ is saying, "Whoever reads that *ṣalawāt* will be as if he read all the *ṣalawāt* of all Creation, including *ins, jinn*, angels, and anything that makes *ṣalawāt* on the Prophet ﷺ." We also said that the Prophet ﷺ will take his hand towards Paradise and bring him into Paradise. At the same time there are billions and billions of Muslims and for the Prophet ﷺ to take them to Paradise, he will take the hands of those who read that *ṣalawāt*.

There are *ṣalawāt* for all different kinds of issues. The *Dalā'il al-Khayrāt* combined all these *ṣalawāt*, it contains all the *ṣalawāt* of *awlīyāullāh* that they received in dreams and visions. As we mentioned the *ḥadīth*:

> *Sayyiduna Abu Hurayrah ؓ reports that the Messenger of Allāh ﷺ said, "He who saw me in a dream has certainly seen me, for Shayṭan can not take my form."* (Bukhari and Muslim)

So *awlīyāullāh* are taking these *ṣalawāt* from the Prophet ﷺ in their dreams, as we mentioned that Imam Bukhari ق was taking the titles of *ḥadīth* after sleeping and seeing Prophet ﷺ in his dream telling him the title and the placement.

(From *The Naqshbandi Guide Book.*) Reading this in your daily *awrād* is to take from Grandshaykh ʿAbdAllāh ق and Great-Grandshaykh Sharafuddin ق, back to Shaykh Abu Aḥmad as-Sughuri ق, and so on. (Shaykh Hisham recites the *Ihda* three times, then this *ṣalawāt*.)

صَلَواتُ اللهِ تعالى ومَلائِكَتِهِ وأنبيائه ورَسُلِهِ وجَميعِ خَلقِهِ على مُحَمَّدٍ وعلى آلِ مُحَمَّدٍ، عليه وعليهِمُ السَّلامُ ورَحْمَةُ اللهِ تَعالى وبَرَكاتُهُ

Salawātullāhi wa malā'ikatihi wa anbiyaihi wa rusūlihi wa jamiʿī khalqihi ʿalā Muḥammad wa ʿalā āli Muḥammad ʿalayhi wa ʿalayhimu 's-salām wa raḥmatullāhi wa barakatuh. (Read 3 times)

Blessings of Allāh Almighty, of His Angels, of His Prophets, of His Messengers, and all Creation be upon Muḥammad and the family of Muḥammad; may the Peace and Mercy of Allāh Almighty and His Blessings be upon upon him and upon them.

Yā Sayyīdinā ʿAlī ﷺ! We read it three times, as you said, "Anyone who reads it three times daily and a hundred times on *Jumuʿah*, it is as if he recited the *ṣalawāt* of all of Creation!" It is like a treasure chest full of gold coins! When you open the box of *ṣalawāt*, it opens the *ṣalawāt* of all Creation as if you read every one and then the Prophet ﷺ will take you by the hand to Paradise!

Then the following was added to that *ṣalawāt*, recited three times:

ʿAlā ashrafi 'l-ʿalamīna Sayyīdinā Muḥammadin ṣalawāt. ʿalā afdali 'l-ʿalamīna Sayyīdinā Muḥammadin ṣalawāt. ʿalā akmali' l-ʿalamīna Sayyīdinā Muḥammadin ṣalawāt.

On the Most Honored of Creation Sayyīdinā Muḥammad prayers. On the Best of Creation Sayyīdinā Muḥammad prayers. On the Most Perfect of Creation Sayyīdinā Muḥammad prayers.

Salawātullāhi wa malā'ikatihi wa anbiyāihi wa rusūlihi wa jamiʿī khalqihi ʿalā Muḥammad wa ʿalā āli Muḥammad ʿalayhi wa ʿalayhimu 's-salām wa raḥmatullāhi wa barakatuh.

Blessings of Allāh Almighty, of His Angels, of His Prophets, of His Messengers, and all Creation be upon Muḥammad and the family of Muḥammad; may the Peace and Mercy of Allāh Almighty and His Blessings be upon upon him and upon them.

Then the next part was added by the Prophet ﷺ in a vision of Shaykh Sharafuddin ق:

> *Wa radi-Allāhu tabaraka wa taʿalā ʿan-sādātinā as-ḥābi rasūlillāhi ajmaʿīn. Wa ʿani 't-tābiʿīna bihim bi-ihsānin, wa ʿani 'l-a'immati 'l-mujtahidīn al-mādīn, wa ʿani 'l-ʿulamāi 'l-muttaqīn, wa ʿani 'l-awliyāi 's-sālihīn, wa ʿan mashayikhinā fi 't-tarīqatin naqshibandiyyati 'l-ʿaliyyah, qaddas Allāhu taʿala arwāhahumu 'z-zakiyya, wa nawwarr Allāhu taʿalā adrihatamu 'l-mubāraka, wa ʿadallāhu taʿalā ʿalaynā min barakātihim wa fuyūdatihim dā'iman wa 'l-hamdulillāhi rabbi 'l-ʿalamīn.*
>
> *May Allāh, the Blessed and Most High, be pleased with every one of our Masters of juristic reasoning, and with the pious scholars, and the righteous saints and with our shaykhs in the exalted Naqshbandi Order. May Allāh ﷻ sanctify their pure souls and illuminate their blessed graves. May Allāh ﷻ return to us of their blessings and overflowing bounty, always. Praise belongs to Allāh, Lord of the Worlds.*

As Grandshaykh ق said, "If you recite that *ṣalawāt* once, it is heavier than if the whole of Creation from the time of Sayyīdinā Adam ﷺ up to Judgment Day was standing twenty-four hours in *ṣalawāt*, and if they finished that they repeated it for another twenty-four hours, and then repeated it then endlessly, and took all their lives and put their *ṣalawāt* on one side of the Scale and the *ṣalawāt* of Grandshaykh Sharafuddin ad-Daghestani ق on the other side, it will be heavier!

Now there are many forms of *ṣalawāt*, but since Sayyīdinā ʿAlī ؓ mentioned that particular *ṣalawāt*, which is in the middle of Shaykh Sharafuddin's *ṣalawāt*, coming from Prophet ﷺ to heart of *awlīyāullāh*, we recite this daily. See how lucky we are! They don't turn us down, but teach us what we need to learn and know!

I will end with this. It is said in the book *Matali al-Mussarrāt*, which mentions some of the sayings of the *Saḥābah* ؓ that there is not a single place in which *ṣalawāt* on the Prophet ﷺ is recited but a sweet scent will rise up from that place reaching to the Heavens, and all Creation will smell that scent except human beings! And that is why we used to read *Dalāʿil al-Khayrāt* in jamaʿat and sat on benches, twenty, seventy or a hundred people, two-hundred people, and in the same voice we recited *Dalāʿil al-Khayrāt,* in the late 1960s, and throughout the 1970s and 1980s.

We once went to Bonovodro Village in Pekalongena, East Java, Indonesia near the home of Shaykh Mustafa, in which the whole city closes an hour before Maghrib, and after *ʿAsr* thousands come to the main masjid that holds thousands of people, and they place microphones on the grass everywhere and they collectively recite *Dalāʿil al-Khayrāt!* They have done this daily for two-hundred years. We got one copy; it is on Sufilive.com. All of them recite in the same tone, like the sound of a swarm of bees. They finish at Maghrib and go. They say they observed that practice since one Yemeni shaykh came there.

The *Saḥābah* ﷺ can see the Prophet ﷺ, the Imams and grandchildren in dreams, *a'immat al ithnā ʿashar,* they can be with the Prophet ﷺ anytime. They said in any place that you are reciting any form of *ṣalawāt*—and the form we mentioned is one of the highest, but any form, even, "*Allāhumma salli ʿalā Muḥammad wa ʿalā āli Muḥammad*"—there will appear a beautiful, heavenly fragrance from the Prophet's beauty that will penetrate the Seven Heavens until it reaches the Throne of Allāh ﷻ! Because every mu'min or Muslim who makes wudu and prays two *rakaʿats* before he sleeps, his soul will ascend in *sajda* under the Throne, and this is an authentic *ḥadīth* of the Prophet ﷺ, so they cannot deny it.

All of Creation will smell that heavenly fragrance except two groups, human beings and *jinn,* who are both liable because of their bad actions. Angels are *maʿsūm,* infallible, and animals and plant life are not judged; trees and animals make *tasbīḥ* and they can smell it. Whatever Allāh ﷻ created can smell that, except those who are on Earth and ins and jinn, who, had they smelled it, life would have stopped, because everyone would be preoccupied with that smell: their life and breath will be that smell, their heart would pump that smell, their thinking would be focused on that smell, their hands would move on that smell, their feet would walk on that smell! That is why Allāh ﷻ did not allow it to be smelled by ins or jinn.

And everything that Allāh created other than ins and jin, meaning angels and whatever Allāh created other than angels, will ask istighfār for these people, and on the number of those making istighfār for you in that association, all will be written for you. If one-million or one-billion are in that association, it is for you. That is why there are levels in Paradise, the

First Heaven, Second Heaven, and above the seven levels of Heaven, Allāh ﷻ knows what is there. Whether there is one person in that majlis or a large number of people doing *ṣalawāt,* they will all get the same amount of rewards, as mentioned in the book *Talkhīs al-Maʿarif,* page 73.

Inshā'Allāh, we will continue more on these issues of *ṣalawāt* on the Prophet ﷺ because Mawlana Shaykh Nazim asked from his representatives in particular that he wants to put a school for teaching only the Greatness of the Prophet ﷺ. So we are, *inshā'Allāh,* doing this program to show the Greatness of the Prophet ﷺ and we are trying through small associations until we are able to make a school in London in our new building, to make a kind of crash course on the Greatness of the Prophet ﷺ. This is a taste of that and you are tasting the sweetness, but there is more!

How to Amend Heedless Actions

Many pious and sincere people have said to recite these *ṣalawāt* is a *kaffarah* (amends wrong actions) and forgiveness for those who missed prayers and fasting in their lives. If you missed prayers and fasting, go back and see it. However, that doesn't mean you don't need to make them up; rather, with every prayer, make up one prayer and also keep the intention of making up all your missed prayers. For those who missed fasting, they can fast Mondays and Thursdays or during winter when days are short, they can fast. To fast on Friday is not recommended. Also, it is easy to fast twelve hours, so find those days and fast then, and it will be *kaffarah,* unless you want to give out *ṣadaqah,* but that is not as easy.

I don't want to stress you out, but if someone intentionally breaks his fast, his *kaffarah* is to fast sixty consecutive days for one day's fast or to give food to sixty people, the cost of one meal per person. So you can do that over the coming years and Allāh ﷻ is The One Who Forgives, so make your intention. What else can you do other than that? You can distribute sixty breads a day in a poor Muslim country, giving one bread to one person and a cup of rice, or one pound of rice and whatever of flour, etc. That will be enough for a whole family. In any case, you can give *kaffarah* money or make intention that you will slowly, slowly make it up, and Allāh will forgive you, *inshā'Allāh.*

I will tell you a story about a rich man in the time of Great-Grandshaykh Sharafuddin ad-Daghestani ق and Grandshaykh ʿAbdAllāh

ق. He was so rich and he was not a practicing Muslim, when suddenly Allāh ﷻ guided him back to the normal practice of Islam and he said, "I am leaving behind all that I did before and am going to be a muʿmin, a Muslim, keeping all my prayers and fasting." He went to many scholars and asked them, "All these years I have not paid *zakāt*. How much do I have to pay now?" Each one said, "One-million golden coins," which disturbed him. You know it is hard to say, "I will pay."

May Allāh ﷻ forgive us, as we have made many mistakes in our payments of *zakāt*, but his ego was not letting him spend half a million or one-million, until finally he came to Grandshaykh ق ʿAbdAllāh, who was young at the time, and said, "What do I have to pay?" Grandshaykh ق said, "I, as khalifah of Shaykh Sharafuddin (who only lived sixty-three years), will make *istikhara*. Come tomorrow and I will give you an answer."

He came the next day and Grandshaykh ق told him, "My *istikhara* showed you only have to pay five-hundred golden coins." That was a huge discount, might be 99% of what he was previously told!

Astonished, that man said, "Is that it?"

Grandshaykh ق said, "That is it and you will be excused." Look how *awlīyāullāh* can manage people! He said, "Okay, I will bring five-hundred golden coins."

Then Grandshaykh said, "No, no, don't give that to me, but bring a drinking water system for the villages." You can see in villages all these taps for water from the Ottoman times.

That man said, "I am going to begin it." After saying that to Grandshaykh ق, that night a dream in which the Prophet ﷺ said to him, "O my son! I accept what my son told you."

That man came running to Grandshaykh ق in his night clothes at *Fajr* time and said, "*Yā Sayyidī*! I saw the Prophet ﷺ saying to me he accepted the five-hundred golden coins. Now I will not give only five hundred, I will give five million!" See how *awlīyāullāh* hook people? That man was so happy to see the Prophet ﷺ! People wish to see the Prophet ﷺ and will give their lives to see him! And then he gave five-million gold coins to supply drinking water to different places in Turkey. So *awlīyāullāh* know.

Now we say, make intention and do your prayers, fasting and good deeds, and when the intention to do that is strong, Allāh ﷻ will see your actions and intentions and forgive you! May Allāh ﷻ forgive us and bless us!

ʿAlā ashrafi ʾl-ʿalamīna Sayyīdinā Muḥammadin ṣalawāt, ʿalā afdali ʾl-ʿalamīna Sayyīdinā Muḥammadin ṣalawāt, ʿalā akmali ʾl-ʿalamīna Sayyīdinā Muḥammadin ṣalawāt. Salawātullāhi wa malāʾikatihi wa anbiyāihi wa rusūlihi wa jamiʿī khalqihi ʿalā Muḥammad wa ʿalā āli Muḥammad ʿalayhi wa ʿalayhimu ʾs-salām wa raḥmatullāhi wa barakātuh.

When you recite this, it is as if you made *ṣalawāt* with all of Creation and the benefit of all that was shared with you!

Say this three times a day and a hundred times on Friday:

Salawātullāhi wa malāʾikatihi wa anbiyāihi wa rusūlihi wa jamiʿī khalqihi ʿalā Muḥammad wa ʿalā āli Muḥammad ʿalayhi wa ʿalayhimu ʾs-salām wa raḥmatullāhi wa barakatuh.

May Allāh ﷻ forgive us and may Allāh ﷻ bless us.

Wa min Allāhi ʿt-tawfiq, bi ḥurmati ʿl-ḥabīb, bi ḥurmati ʿl-Fātiḥah.

And with Allāh is success. For the sake of the Beloved, for his sake we recite the opening chapter of Holy Qur'an.

The Prophet's Love is with Awliyaullah

Aʿūdhu billāhi min ash-Shayṭāni 'r-rajīm. Bismillāhi' r-Raḥmāni 'r-Raḥīm.
Nawaytu 'l-arbāʿīn, nawaytu 'l-ʿitikāf, nawaytu'l-khalwah, nawaytu 'l-ʿuzlah,
nawaytu 'r-riyāḍa, nawaytu 's-sulūk, lillāhi Taʿalā fī hādhā 'l-masjid.
Atīʿūllāha wa atīʿū 'r-Rasūla wa ūlī 'l-amri minkum.
Obey Allāh, obey the Prophet, and obey those in authority among you. (4:59)

Dastūr, madad yā Sulṭān al-Awlīyā, Mawlana Shaykh Nazim al-Haqqani ق.
Dastūr, madad yā Sulṭān al-Awlīyā, Mawlana Shaykh ʿAbdAllāh ad-Daghestani ق.

I have opened a book here, because I heard Mawlana say many times that he wished that all around the world scholars would speak about the greatness of Sayyīdinā Muḥammad ﷺ, how he is different from everyone else and has been respected by Allāh ﷻ and His angels. So I brought this book to mention something from it about the greatness of Sayyīdinā Muḥammad ﷺ and how up to today many scholars and *awlīyāullāh* from around the world have been respecting and loving him, and encouraging their followers to give more and more love and respect to him ﷺ.

And just to say, I am speaking by the order of Mawlana Shaykh Nazim and taking permission from Shaykh Mehmet, who is the representative of Mawlana Shaykh Nazim al-Haqqani ق.

I will begin by mentioning one *ḥadīth* that stresses the importance of loving the Prophet ﷺ.

One time a Bedouin came to the Prophet ﷺ while he was on the *minbar* giving *khutbah.* He came to the door of the *masjid* and said, "*Yā* Muḥammad!" You know the desert Bedouins are sometimes rude in the way they talk; their life is hard and they can be very direct, so he said, "*Yā* Muḥammad!" he didn't say, "*Yā Rasūlullāh*!" The Prophet ﷺ was in *Jumuʿah* and didn't answer. Then he asked a second time, "*Yā* Muḥammad! When is Judgment Day?" And the Prophet ﷺ didn't answer out of *adab* to Allāh ﷻ that this is the *Jumuʿah.* Then the Bedouin asked the third time, "When is Judgment Day?"

Then Jibrīl ﷺ came to the Prophet ﷺ and said, "Answer him," so Prophet ﷺ answered him, saying, "What have you prepared for that long journey?"

Life is a journey; you might live ten, fifty or one-hundred years, but what have you prepared for that journey? It is not easy.

In another *ḥadīth*, Prophet ﷺ asked the *Saḥābah* ﷺ, "Who is the bankrupt, poor one who has nothing?" The *Saḥābah* ﷺ said, "The one who has no money." The Prophet ﷺ said, "No, the one who has no *ʿamal* is poor." And they said, "Even if he fasts and prays?" He said, "Yes, even if he fasts and prays."

The Prophet ﷺ said:

Do you know who the muflis (bankrupt one) is? The muflis from my Ummah is one who comes on the Day of Judgment having performed prayer, fasting, and giving zakāt. However, along with all of this, he abused this person and slandered that person, ate the wealth of this person and unlawfully spilled the blood of that person. These people will take from his good deeds. If, however, his good deeds become exhausted, then their sins will be put upon him and he will be thrown into the Fire. (Muslim)

So being "bankrupt" is due to many incidents that happen in our life and instead of covering them, we are exposing them. We may hear something and it might be a mistake, but we bring down the respect of that man or woman. So the Prophet ﷺ taught us to always have good intentions, good thoughts, and to look more at the positive, not at the negative. If that person has mistakes, look to see is he more positive and if he is, cover the mistake and overlook it.

So the Prophet ﷺ asked that Bedouin, "O ʿArabi! Did you pray and fast? Did you not spread false rumors and backbite people? Did you prepare to be a good and lovable person? Did you audit and check yourself before checking others?"

Let us check ourselves before we check others to see are we on the right path or wrong path. *Alḥamdulillāh,* we are on the right path of Mawlana Shaykh Nazim and we are following him, may Allāh ﷻ support him, give him health, honor him and show his power in front of the Prophet ﷺ! But that does not mean we have to refrain from what has to be said, not in the way of complaining and putting someone in the corner, but rather in the way of giving good advice. So let us audit ourselves before we complain about our brothers and sisters. That applies to all of us, to you and to me.

There is only one who is perfect: the Prophet ﷺ! Allāh ﷻ has protected Sayyīdinā Muḥammad ﷺ and all other Prophets, as they are *maʿsūm,* infallible. Although the brothers of Sayyīdinā Yusuf ؑ who were also Prophets put him in the well, still they are *maʿsūm;* they were drawn to do those acts to show the greatness of Sayyīdinā Yusuf ؑ. Similarly, for *Saḥābah* ؓ, of whom we don't speak badly, or for great *shuyūkh,* for whom respect is to respect their followers, we must also respect each other. To love Mawlana Shaykh Nazim is easy, but we also have to love each other. So that *ḥadīth* of the Arab coming from the desert is important.

The Prophet ﷺ asked him, "What have you prepared?"

He had not prepared anything, so he said, "I love you, *yā Rasūlullāh*!"

The Signs of Real Love

The word "love" in Arabic is "*hubb*." Many people speak about *hubb*; they say, "love, love, love." You might love a girl more than your father and mother. Is that real love? Where is your father and your mother (in that love)? Or you might love your son more than yourself; is that real love?

Hubb consists of two letters, "*Hā*," which represents "*hayāt*," life and the beauty of life in loving Allāh ﷻ and His Prophet ﷺ and the *Saḥābah* ؓ. "*Bā*" represents "*baqa*," which means "existence that never disappears." Therefore, "*hubb*" also means "life" and "existence." When you reach *fanāʿ*, the state of complete annihilation in the Divine Presence of Allāh ﷻ, the Prophet ﷺ and in the shaykh, that will take you to *baqa*.

When you annihilate, your shaykh takes you to real existence and that makes you like a spotlight, a magnet that attracts people. That is *hubb*: *fanāʿ* and *baqa*. When you love someone you annihilate in them and even if he kicks you out from the door, you come in again from the window. Grandshaykh ق said many times, "If I kick you from the door, come from the window. If I kick you from the window, come from the ceiling!"

Don't have bad feelings about the shaykh, who is a mirror. When you look in the mirror it reflects your character. The shaykh also has representatives and they are like him, so when you look at them you see your own character, not the representative's character. That is your own character you are seeing there.

Al-mu'min mirrāt akhīhi.

The believer is the mirror of his brother (or sister).

You don't see him, you see yourself, so you are seeing your own characters. When you see his good character it means yours is good, and if you see his bad character then yours is bad, and it might not be one-to-one, as always Shayṭan might play with the mirror to give you a bad feeling about that person. Therefore, we must always say *"astaghfirullāh."* When the Bedouin asked, "When is Judgment Day?" the Prophet ﷺ said, "What did you prepare for that? Did you audit yourself?" We counted seventeen major categories of bad manners when we look at the self. Some of them are stinginess, pride, anger, love of *dunya,* and you need to get rid of them. These obstacles are in front of you and yet you claim you love. Actually, you don't love, you have pain.

And the Bedouin said from a real heart, "I love you with my life! I give my life to you, *yā* Muḥammad!" How many times did the *Saḥābah* say, "I give my life to you, *yā* Muḥammad, and the life of my father and mother!" That is real love. At that time they will reach *baqa,* existence in the Divine Presence, not to disappear. So the love of the Prophet ﷺ is with *awlīyāullāh,* and we want to establish this while I am here because I will make this a series of talks.

Also, we want to mention something to help us better understand. They might say, "Everyone is a *wali,*" or "Every *mu'min* is a *wali.*" So who is a *wali*? In that *ḥadīth,* it is said that a person might be bankrupt of deeds even if he prays and fasts. So we need to establish what is meant by *"wali."* What is the best or most-read book after the Holy Qur'an, from the *sihah* books? Is it not the book of Imam Muḥammad Ismaʿīl Bukhari ؓ, the *Saḥih al-Bukhari*? Every *ḥadīth* he found, first he verified it; he didn't write the *ḥadīth* until he made *istikhara,* even if he travelled hundreds of miles to get that *ḥadīth.* Then he slept and would get the answer. This process is established by all scholars, Ahl as-*Sunnah* wa 'l-Jama'ah and even Wahhabis, that he would see a dream of the Prophet ﷺ, who would confirm that *ḥadīth.*

The form of the Prophet ﷺ cannot be taken by Shayṭan, so whoever saw the Prophet ﷺ in a dream saw him in reality and will see him in reality! So whatever the Prophet ﷺ said to someone in a dream, that is *haqq* and that person cannot lie. No Muslim can see the Prophet ﷺ and lie about it, saying, "I saw the Prophet ﷺ," although they didn't, because he would feel bad. As in the Holy Qur'an, we see that many times where Allāh ﷻ sent dreams. We say "dream," but for the Prophets it is a vision as in the case of Sayyīdinā Ibrahim ﷺ and Sayyīdinā Isma'īl ﷺ, and so on. So when *awlīyāullāh* see something by vision or dreams they cannot lie about that.

Each *wali* has different highways. There are 124,000 *awlīyāullāh* and each one has a different way, but for us, Mawlana Shaykh Nazim is our *Sultan ul-Awlīyā,* and we are on his way, which is a big highway!

Salawat Dictated from Prophet

Long ago, one *wali,* Shaykh Muḥammad al-Talmaysani ق, saw the Prophet ﷺ in a dream. He had read *Dalā'il al-Khayrāt* 100,000 times and then he saw the Prophet ﷺ in the dream, saying to him, "*Yā* Muḥammad! If you read this *ṣalawāt,* it will be as if you read *Dalā'il al-Khayrāt* 800,000 times!"

It is the recitation of Sayyīdinā Aḥmad al-Badawi:

Salawat Nuraniyyah/Salawat Badawi Kubra

اَللّٰهُمَّ صَلِّ وَسَلِّمْ وَبَارِكْ عَلَى سَيِّدِنَا وَمَوْلَانَا مُحَمَّدٍ شَجَرَةِ الأَصْلِ النُّوْرَانِيَّةِ، وَلَمْعَةِ الْقَبْضَةِ الرَّحْمَانِيَّةِ، وَأَفْضَلِ الْخَلِيْقَةِ الاِنْسَانِيَّةِ، وَأَشْرَفِ الصُّوْرَةِ الْجِسْمَانِيَّةِ، وَمَعْدِنِ الأَسْرَارِ الرَّبَّانِيَّةِ، وَخَزَائِنِ الْعُلُوْمِ الاِصْطِفَائِيَّةِ، صَاحِبِ الْقَبْضَةِ الأَصْلِيَّةِ، وَالْبَهْجَةِ السَّنِيَّةِ، وَالرُّتْبَةِ الْعَلِيَّةِ، مَنِ انْدَرَجَتِ النَّبِيُّوْنَ تَحْتَ لِوَائِهِ، فَهُمْ مِنْهُ وَاِلَيْهِ، وَصَلِّ وَسَلِّمْ وَبَارِكْ عَلَيْهِ وَعَلَى آلِهِ وَصَحْبِهِ عَدَدَ مَاخَلَقْتَ، وَرَزَقْتَ وَأَمَتَّ وَأَحْيَيْتَ اِلَى يَوْمِ تَبْعَثُ مَنْ أَفْنَيْتَ، وَسَلِّمْ تَسْلِيْمًاكَثِيْرًا وَالْحَمْدُ لِلّٰهِ رَبِّ الْعَالَمِيْنَ.

Allāhumma salli wa sallim wa bārik 'ala Sayyīdinā wa Mawlana Muḥammadin shajarati 'l-aslin nūrāniyyati wa lam'atil qabdati 'r-raḥmāniyyati wa afdali 'l-khalīqati 'l-insāniyyati wa ashrafi 's-sūrati 'l-jismāniyyati wa m'adini 'l-asrāri 'r-rabBanīyyati wa khazāini 'l 'ulūmi 'l-istifāiyyati, sāḥibi 'l-qabdati 'l-asliyya wa 'l-bahjati 's-saniyya wa 'r-rutbatil 'aliyya, manin darajati 'n-nabiyyūna tahtali wāihi, fahum minhu wa ilayhi, wa salli wa sallim wa bārik 'alayhi wa 'ala ālihi wa sāḥbihi 'adada mā khalaqta wa razaqta wa amatta wa ahyayta ilā yawmi tabʿathu man afnayta wa sallim taslīman kathīra wa 'l-hamdulillāhi rabbi 'l-ʿalamīn.

O Allāh! Bless, greet and sanctify our master and liegelord Muḥammad ﷺ, the Tree of Original Light, the Sparkle of the Handful of Divine Mercy, the Best of All Humankind, the Noblest of Physical Frames, the Vessel of the Lord's Secrets and Storehouse of the Sciences of the Elect, the Possessor of the Original Divine Grasp, Resplendent Grace, and Uppermost Rank, under whose flag line up all the Prophets, so that they are from him and point to him. Bless, greet and sanctify him and his Family and Companions, to the number of all that You have ever created, sustained, caused to die and caused to live again, to the Day You resurrect those You reduced to dust, and greet him with an abundant and endless greeting. Glory and praise belong to Allāh, the Lord of the Worlds!

We just read it now the way it was given by Prophet ﷺ to Muḥammad al-Talmaysani ق, and it is as if we read *Dalāʿil al-Khayrāt* 100,000 times. The *dalīl* is from Sayyīdinā ʿAlī ق and this is in the book *Nahj al-Mutaqqīn*, and it says because they are *awlīyāullāh* and it is established by what the Prophet ﷺ said to them as they see Prophet ﷺ in their dreams, it means they saw him correctly because Shayṭan cannot imitate the Prophet's image.

The *ḥadīth* mentioned, *sa yarānī*, "You will see me." Imam Suyuti ؓ said, "That means you will Prophet ﷺ him in *dunya*. It would not refer to *Akhirah*, because everyone will see the Prophet ﷺ in *Akhirah*."

Also, if you recite that *ṣalawāt* three times daily and one-hundred times on *Jumuʿah*, it will be as if you have performed the worship of all human beings since the time they were created up to Judgment Day! How many human beings are there? How big is the *ummah* of the Prophet ﷺ? In one dream or vision, Grandshaykh ʿAbdAllāh al-Fa'iz ad-Daghestani ق said that the Prophet ﷺ said to him, "My *ummah* is 400 billion people." That is *ummat an-Nabī* ﷺ! In this century it is 1.5 billion. If you add them all up, from the time of Sayyīdinā Adam ؑ to today, it is 400 billion! There is a *ḥadīth* about that where the Prophet ﷺ said, "My *ummah* is 70,000 times 70,000 times 70,000," which is nearly 400 billion, coinciding with what Grandshaykh ق said.

So if you read that *ṣalawāt*, (the reward) is on the number of the *ummah*, which is 400 billion, as Sayyīdinā ʿAlī ؓ said, "It is on the number of all

Creation, including the number of non-Muslims, from the time of Adam ﷺ." It is a huge number! Who recites this three times a day and one-hundred times on the day of *Jumu'ah* will be raised on Judgment Day with the Prophet ﷺ, who will take his hand until he takes him to his place in Paradise!

I was curious since a long time ago, because Grandshaykh ق and Mawlana Shaykh Nazim ق ordered us to read a *ṣalawāt*: *'ala ashraf al-'ālamīna Sayyīdinā Muḥammad* ﷺ *ṣalawāt, 'ala akmalil-'ālamīna Sayyīdinā Muḥammad ṣalawāt, 'ala afdal'il-'ālamīna Sayyīdinā Muḥammad* ﷺ *ṣalawāt*. And I looked through many books and never found that *ḥadīth* of Sayyīdinā 'Alī ؓ until I found it in *Nahj al-Mutaqqīn*:

صَلَواتُ اللهِ تعالى ومَلائِكَتِهِ وأنبيائه ورُسُلِهِ وجَميع خَلْقِهِ على مُحَمَّدٍ وعلى آل مُحَمَّدٍ، عليه وعليهمُ السَّلامُ ورَحْمَةُ اللهِ تَعالى وبَرَكاتُهُ

Ṣalawātullāhi wa malā'ikatihi wa anbiyāihi wa rusūlihi wa jami'ī khalqihi 'alā Muḥammad wa 'alā āli Muḥammad 'alayhi wa 'alayhimu 's-salām wa raḥmatullāhi wa barakatuh.

Blessings of Allāh Almighty, of His Angels, of His Prophets, of His Messengers, and all Creation be upon Muḥammad and the family of Muḥammad; may the Peace and Mercy of Allāh Almighty and His Blessings be upon him and upon them.

That is part of the *ṣalawāt* that Mawlana Shaykh Nazim told us to recite every day or after each prayer, because this allows us to take the hands of the Prophet ﷺ, who will take us into our place in Paradise!

روى الإمام أحمد في صحيحه عن أم المؤمنين السيدة عائشة رضي الله تعالى عنها أن رسول الله قال : "إنه خلق كل إنسان من بني آدم على ستين وثلاثمائة مفصل فمن كبر الله وحمد الله وسبح الله واستغفر الله وعزل حجراً من طريق الناس أو شوكة أو عظماً عن طريق الناس وأمر بالمعروف ونهى عن منكر عدد تلك الستين والثلاثمائة سلامى فإنه يمشي يومئذ وقد زحزح عن النار"مسلم

'Ayesha ؓ reported Allāh's Messenger ﷺ as saying: Every one of the children of Adam has been created with 360 joints; so he who declares the Glory of Allāh, praises Allāh, declares Allāh to be One, Glorifies Allāh, and seeks forgiveness from Allāh, and removes a stone or thorn or a bone from people's

path, and enjoins what is good and forbids from evil, to the number of those 360 (joints) will walk that day having removed himself from Hell.

(*Saḥih Muslim*, Book 005, Number 2199)

May Allāh ﷻ forgive us and may Allāh ﷻ bless us.

Wa min Allāhi 't-tawfiq, bi ḥurmati 'l-ḥabīb, bi ḥurmati 'l-Fātiḥah.

And with Allāh is success. For the sake of the Beloved, for his sake we recite the opening chapter of Holy Qur'an.

Scientific Truths Rooted in Ahadith

Aʿūdhu billāhi min ash-Shayṭāni 'r-rajīm. Bismillāhi' r-Raḥmāni 'r-Raḥīm.
Nawaytu 'l-arbāʿīn, nawaytu 'l-ʿitikāf, nawaytu'l-khalwah, nawaytu 'l-ʿuzlah,
nawaytu 'r-riyāḍa, nawaytu 's-sulūk, lillāhi Taʿālā fī hādhā 'l-masjid.
Atīʿūllāha wa atīʿū 'r-Rasūla wa ūlī 'l-amri minkum.
Obey Allāh, obey the Prophet, and obey those in authority among you. (4:59)

Dastūr, madad yā Sulṭān al-Awlīyā, Mawlana Shaykh Nazim al-Haqqani ق.
Dastūr, madad yā Sulṭān al-Awlīyā, Mawlana Shaykh ʿAbdAllāh ad-Daghestani ق.

We are asking for support from the Prophet ﷺ because we are speaking about Islam, which is the message of Sayyīdinā Muḥammad ﷺ. Clearly, we have to establish a solid base to limit any confusion about what we are saying in these sessions.

A few days ago, some people sent me a message that workers were digging deep to make a five-star hotel in Riyadh. They reached what was like a grave, omitting a very lovely fragrance. With caution, they tried digging slowly and they found two shrouded bodies that were still fresh with fresh faces, as if they had just been buried. Everything about them was fresh, and if you touched them they were soft and light was coming from their eyes. They immediately stopped the excavation. They brought scientists to determine how many years the bodies had been there, and the scientific analysis revealed the two bodies were buried next to each other more than 300-400 years ago!

Then told me the head of Religious Affairs for that area came and looked, and he was amazed because in that area of Riyadh, or anywhere in Saudi Arabia, if you bury someone they decompose in thirty days die to the sun's heat. Those bodies had not decomposed, which prompted him to declare that they are "pious people"; he didn't say they are "*awlīyāullāh,*" but "pious people whom Allāh ﷻ rewarded by preserving their bodies". Upon hearing this news, crowds assembled to visit those graves and the government closed that place.

That incident is to establish that *awlīyāullāh* do exist and when they die, as the Prophet ﷺ said:

Hayātī khayrun lakum tuḥadīthūna wa yuhdatha lakum fa idhā anā mitta kānat wafātī khayran lakum. Tuʿradu ʿalayya ʿamālakum fa in rā'itu khayran hamadt 'Llāh taʿala wa in rā'itu sharran astaghfarta lakum.

My life is good for you as you will relate from me and it will be related to you, and when I die my passing will be better for you. (Meaning, "My death is better for you than my life, because then I can pray for you.") *I observe the ʿamal of my ummah. If I see good I thank Allāh the Exalted, and if I see evil I ask forgiveness for you.*

So this *ummah* is an *ummah* that has been forgiven. Also, there are *awlīyāullāh* to whom Allāh ﷻ has given the ability to see the Prophet ﷺ in dreams, and even many normal people see the Prophet ﷺ in dreams, is it not? The Prophet ﷺ said, "Who saw me in the dream saw me right (actually saw me)." So it means whatever you ask in the dream and what Prophet ﷺ answers is correct, as explained previously. *Awlīyāullāh* experience visions and dreams in which they see the Prophet ﷺ and they tell the people about it.

I brought a book titled, *Al-ʿAqd as-Samīn*, which quotes Sayyīdinā ʿAlī ؓ. You may ask, why did I bring a book and not speak directly? I can speak directly, it is not an issue, but what is the benefit if you don't quote *ḥadīth* and the references? You might say I am speaking of imaginary things and calling it "inspirations"! Many people I know do that, and I am not speaking of Mawlana Shaykh's representatives, but many non-representatives begin to speak and then say it is from the shaykh. No, you did something wrong. Sayyīdinā Adam ؑ said to Allāh ﷻ, "What is good is from You and what I did of bad is from me." However, Iblīs said, "What I did wrong is from You." So don't say it is a test! If you made a mistake, admit it and ask for forgiveness.

So I brought this book so that if people ask they can know, and we are speaking primarily of people on the Internet, because the people here with us accept whatever I say and they will say, "Yes, that is right." Some viewers on the Internet don't accept that as they might be on a different road that is not ours, or maybe they have a different shaykh or they do not accept *ḥadīth*[3],. That is why we make sure what we say is recorded and then we say in addition to it.

> *Fi 'l-qawli 'l-badī'ī 'an 'aliyyin 'an an-nabiyy ﷺ qāla man hajj hajjat al-Islam wa ghazā ba'dahā ghazwatan katabat ghazwatahu bi-arba' mi'at hajjah fa-ankasarat qulūbi qawmun lā yaqdirūna 'alā al-jihād fa-awḥā-Llāhu ilayhi mā salla 'alayka ahadin illa katabat ṣalātahu bi-arba' mi'at ghazwatin arba' mi'at hajjah.*

In the book "*al-Qawl al-Badi'ī*" it is related from Sayyīdinā 'Alī ؓ that the Prophet ﷺ said:

> Whoever did the obligated Hajj of Islam and after that fought in a battle (of jihad), Allāh will write for him 400 pilgrimages. (Upon hearing this) the hearts of those who could not afford to go for jihad were broken, and Allāh ﷻ revealed to Prophet ﷺ, "None of you makes ṣalawāt on you except that it will be written as if he struggled in the Way of Allāh 400 years of jihad and I will reward him 400 pilgrimages.
>
> (Narrated by Abu Hafz in *Majalis al-Makkiyya*)

At that time there was war between believers and unbelievers, who would have killed Muslims had they gone to *Sunnah*. So the Prophet ﷺ said, "Who will go for jihad in the Way of Allāh?" Here "jihad" does not mean suicide bombers, which is terrorism and we don't accept that. He means it will be written for those who go for jihad in the Way of Allāh as those who struggle against unbelievers who aggressively come against the Muslims. But also it can mean if you are engaged in a struggle to educate others or to build something good, "it will be written as if you completed four-hundred *Hajj*," as written in the book, *The Precious String*.

Some people were heartbroken when he said that, because they could not go for *Sunnah*, as Allāh ﷻ said it is for those who can afford it, so those who could not afford it cried, and then Allāh ﷻ revealed to the Prophet ﷺ, who said to Sayyīdinā 'Alī ؓ:

---

[3] The "*Quraniyoon,*" a large group primarily located in Egypt, only accepts what is written in the Holy Qur'an and not the *ḥadīth* of Prophet.

None of you makes ṣalawāt on the Prophet except that it will be written as if he struggled in the Way of Allāh 400 years of jihad and I will reward him 400 pilgrimages.

That is for making one *ṣalawāt* on the Prophet ﷺ! And also the Prophet ﷺ said:

Whoever makes ṣalawāt on me, giving me my rights as the Prophet, then Allāh will make from his ṣalawāt one angel with one wing in the east and one in the west, that makes istighfār up to the Day of Judgment." That istighfār and ṣalawāt is written in the notebook of that person! See how much Allāh ﷻ is giving for the greatness of the Prophet ﷺ! Therefore, zayyinū majālisakum bid-dhikr aw ṣalawāt, ornament your gatherings with dhikr or ṣalawāt!

Fingers that Bear Witness and Points of the Body

Now we come to something that most Muslims have stopped doing, even among *Ahlu 's-Sunnah wa 'l-Jamaʿah.* They uphold this custom mostly in the Sub-continent and in very few other countries. When we call the *adhān* and we come to, *"ash-hadu anna Muḥammad ar-Rasūlullāh,"* we hold our two fingers together, kiss them and say, *qurrati ʿaynī bika yā Rasūlullāh,* "You are the coolness of my eyes, *yā Rasūlullāh*!" The *shahādah* (index) finger and the thumbprint that bears your identity bear witness! Every fingerprint is made of points that contain one's unique code, the connection of different points in different ways, and no individual's fingerprint resembles another. Everyone has different points connecting with the thumb and the *shahādah* finger. So when you do that you are saying, *"Yā Rabbī*! With the name (identity) You gave me, I witness that You are Allāh and that Sayyīdinā Muḥammad is your Messenger!"

Why do you put your fingers on your two eyes? Today scientists have found that everyone's iris is unique, so you are witnessing with your eyes (iris), which is a small point, so don't joke about points and say they don't exist. We must be aware and keep an open mind. We are not Buddhists, but they took their knowledge of points from Islam, which contains all knowledge!

إِنَّ الدِّينَ عِندَ اللهِ الإِسْلامُ

Inna ad-dīna 'inda Allāhi al-islām.

The religion in Allāh's view is Islam (submission to His Will).

(Sūrat Āli-'Imrān, 3:19)

Islam is the perfect religion; even Buddhists took from Islam! If they are putting their hands like that, they learned it from Sayyīdinā Abu Bakr as-Siddiq ؓ, who kissed his fingers and put them on his eyes! So the iris is a point and also an important witness to what you say. That is why the Prophet ﷺ recommends to move every finger across every part of your body, because if your body is moved, all the different points of your body will be moved.

I am not bringing this knowledge about points; Prophet ﷺ said this. If anyone is using points, like an acupuncturist or a physical therapist, what do they do? Why do you go to them? They find points and press on them. So the evidence about points is in this book, *Aja'z fi Ḥadīth al-Mafasil, The Miracle of the Prophet ﷺ in the Joints/Points*, as narrated by Imam Muslim.

Also, Grandshaykh ق and Mawlana Shaykh Nazim ق said there are five points in the heart: *qalb, sirr, sirr as-sirr, khafa, akhfa*. That is recorded in Naqshbandi books and in books of other *ṭarīqahs*, all of which know there are seven points on the chest called *"latā'if,"* and these *ṭarīqas* have mentioned how to move them as the Prophet ﷺ mentioned it. Here are all the names of the lineage of this *ḥadīth* of Imam Muslim, that the Prophet ﷺ said:

> *Every one of the children of Adam has been created with 360 joints; so he who declares the Glory of Allāh, praises Allāh, declares Allāh to be One, Glorifies Allāh, and seeks forgiveness from Allāh, and removes an obstacle from people's path and enjoins what is good and forbids from evil, to the number of those 360 joints or points, will walk that day toward Paradise, having removed himself from Hell.* (Saḥīh Muslim)

Allāh ﷻ created every human being from Adam's descendants on 360 joints, or points. That was mentioned 1,500 years ago. They have never reached 360. It is still a miracle, so where are the others? Whoever makes *takbīr* or praises Allāh ﷻ and makes *tasbīḥ* and removes a stone from the road or anything that might make an accident on the road from the path of people, or who called for good or prevented what is bad every day, *takbir, tahmīd, tahlīl, istighfār,* on the number of 360 points, will have removed himself that day from Hellfire!

That is the *ḥadīth* of the Prophet ﷺ, not from me. That is evidence of the Prophet ﷺ that he mentioned in *Saḥih Muslim, Kitāb az-Zakāt.*

In the *Musnad* of Imam Muslim, it is narrated that the Prophet ﷺ said, *Fi 'l-insān 360 mifsal,* "In the human beings there are 360 points." *Fa ʿalayhi an yatasadaq ʿala kullin minhum sadaqa,* "He has to give a *sadaqa* on every point." So that is why our *shuyūkh* ordered us to put a box by the door so that when you go out you make *sadaqa* and when you come in you put *sadaqa*; that is for your body. Physical therapists press these points. If you don't have money to make *sadaqa,* then do something good, such as help someone or take something from the road or smile in the face of someone as all that is *sadaqa.*

"What if you cannot do that?" they asked the Prophet ﷺ, and he answered, "If you can pray two *rakaʿats Duha,* it is as if you touched these 360 points." And so we pray two *rakaʿats Duha,* and I know you mostly pray four or eight *rakaʿats,* but just two *rakaʿats* will take over all these points. That is why prayer in Islam moves your whole body completely. If you pray two *rakaʿats* you move here, here, here, head, hands, etc. And so when you move everything, it as if you are pressing these 360 points.

Some doctors read this *ḥadīth* and studied the body because they wanted to understand this knowledge. They counted how many points are in the body and they made this list with various categories and titled it *"Al-Mafasil al-ʿAmud al-Fakhdh Walhad."*[4] They added all the points throughout the body, and determined in the vertebrae and hips there are 76 points. When people do massage they press on the vertebrae and move 76 points. We are not Buddhists and we are not throwing words about points, but the Prophet ﷺ is teaching us about them.

Look at the greatness of the Prophet ﷺ! We are bringing this information to show the greatness of Sayyīdinā Muḥammad ﷺ, that 1500 years ago he said the body has 360 points, and Buddhists and others did not

---

[4] You can see this document with names of the researchers and the totals of points in the body online at http://tl.gd/gk2o61.

know about it; they took that knowledge from Islam. That is a miracle of the Holy Qur'an and if we want to go into that, I have a book on that topic, but we cannot elaborate every *ayah*.

Sanurīhim ayātinā fi 'l-āfāq wa fi anfusihim.

We are going to show them Our Signs in the horizons and in themselves.

(Sūrat al-Fussilat, 41:53)

In time of the Prophet ﷺ, he didn't bring this up but he left it to the end of the *ummah,* giving us signs, and this is the *ḥadīth* of the Prophet ﷺ about points. It is not as if I am bringing it from nowhere, it is a fact. And about the hands, although we don't say to do that, people kiss their fingertips and put them to their eyes when they hear the Prophet's holy name. My uncle, the Head of Religious Affairs Dept. in Lebanon, did that. We are not following Hindus or Buddhists, so I am sorry if you heard (what we said) wrong, because there are many people who whisper wrong.

This is the lesson today on evidence of the Greatness of the Prophet ﷺ and we will continue this topic later.

Sayyidina Adam Gave Forty Years of His Life

I would like to mention this *saḥih ḥadīth* from Saḥih Tirmidhi, narrated by Abu Hurayrah ؓ that the Prophet ﷺ said:

Lama khalaqAllāhu adama massaha zhahrahu, "When Allāh created Adam, He stroked his back, which dripped all that Allāh ﷻ created up to the Day of Judgment from his offspring (and) all of them came down. And he made between every human being a ray of light that comes out, wabīsun min nūr, and then he showed them to Adam. That is one meaning of the verse, "And He taught Adam the names of all things." (2:31) *Sayyīdinā Adam* ؑ *said, "Who are these?" Allāh ﷻ said, "Those are your offspring." Sayyīdinā Adam* ؑ *saw one among them and liked the light coming from his eyes, and he asked, "Who is that one?" Allāh ﷻ said, "That is a man named Dawūd from the last of nations from among your descendants." He asked, "O my Lord! How many years of life did You give him?" Allāh ﷻ said, "Sixty years." Sayyīdinā Adam* ؑ *said, "O my Lord! zidhu min ʿumrī, Give him forty years from my life to extend his life." Allāh ﷻ granted that and it was finished. When the Angel of*

Death came to Sayyidinā Adam to take his soul, he said, "O Azrā'īl! Why are you taking my soul, as I still have forty years of life?" The Angel of Death said, "Didn't you ask Allāh to give that one forty years from your life? That is why it is forty years less." Sayyidinā Adam forgot all of that and the Angel of Death reminded him. Fa nasiya Adam wa nasiy dhurriyatahu, "Adam made a mistake and all his descendants make mistakes." Sayyidinā Adam forgot and all the offspring after him also forgot.

That is why many things don't stay in our minds. It is good if you don't remember everything or you would always carry your problems! That is a true and valid *ḥadīth*.

May Allāh forgive us and may Allāh accept us to be with Mawlana Shaykh Nazim, who, in his bed, in his sitting and standing and in his every movement, remembers us and prays for us in the presence of the Prophet! *Yā fawzan li 'l-mustaghfirīn, astaghfirullāh.*

May Allāh bless all of you. This has been to show the Greatness of the Prophet through his *aḥadīth*, that after 1500 years people hear what he said, remember it and see it through their own eyes!

May Allāh forgive us and may Allāh bless us.

Wa min Allāhi 't-tawfīq, bi ḥurmati 'l-ḥabīb, bi ḥurmati 'l-Fātiḥah.
And with Allāh is success. For the sake of the Beloved, for his sake we recite the opening chapter of Holy Qur'an.

Creation of Sayyidina Muhammad's Light

A'ūdhu billāhi min ash-Shayṭāni 'r-rajīm. Bismillāhi' r-Raḥmāni 'r-Raḥīm.
Nawaytu 'l-arbā'īn, nawaytu 'l-'itikāf, nawaytu'l-khalwah, nawaytu 'l-'uzlah, nawaytu 'r-riyāḍa, nawaytu 's-sulūk, lillāhi Ta'alā fī hādhā 'l-masjid.
Atī'ūllāha wa atī'ū 'r-Rasūla wa ūlī 'l-amri minkum.
Obey Allāh, obey the Prophet, and obey those in authority among you. (4:59)

Dastūr, madad yā Sulṭān al-Awlīyā, Mawlana Shaykh Nazim al-Haqqani ق.
Dastūr, madad yā Sulṭān al-Awlīyā, Mawlana Shaykh 'AbdAllāh ad-Daghestani ق.

Today people are discovering many miracles that were related by the Prophet ﷺ 1500 years ago, and one very important knowledge Allāh ﷻ mentioned in Holy Qur'an:

Yā ayyuha 'n-nāsu 't-taqū rabbakumu 'Llādhī khalaqakum min nafsin wāhidatin wa khalaqa minha zawjahā wa baththa minhumā rijālan kathīran wa nisā w 'attaqullāhā 'Llādhī tasa'alūna bihi wa 'l-arhāma inna 'Llāha kāna 'alaykum raqība.

O Mankind! Fear your Lord, Who created you from one soul and created from it its mate and dispersed from both of them many men and women.

(Sūrat an-Nisa, 4:1)

"Allāh ﷻ has created you from one soul, *wa khalaqa minhā zawjahā*, and created from its mate." When Allāh ﷻ created human beings, He ordered Sayyīdinā Jibrīl ؑ to go to the Earth and bring a handful of soil from there. When he brought it to Paradise it was one piece and that is why Allāh ﷻ said in Holy Qur'an, *khalaqakum min nafsin wāhida*, "He created you from one soul." So it means what they are saying today in the Theory of Evolution, that everything came from one cell, was mentioned by Allāh ﷻ in the Holy Qur'an 1500 years ago: Allāh ﷻ created Sayyīdinā Adam ؑ from one handful of soil that Jibrīl ؑ brought from Earth to Paradise, which was that "one cell."

Allāh ﷻ said:

Yā ayyuha an-nabiyyu inna arsalnāka shāhidan wa mubashshiran wa nadhīran wa daʿīan ila Allāhi bi-idhnihi wa sirājan munīra.

O Prophet! Truly We have sent thee as a witness, a bearer of glad tidings and warner, and as one who invites to Allāh by His Leave, and as a Lamp spreading Light. (Sūrat al-Ahzab 33:45-46)

He didn't say, "We are going to send you," but He said it in the past tense, "We <u>sent</u> you as a witness, *shāhidan*." A witness on what? It means witnessing the whole Creation.

The Prophet ﷺ said:

Kunutu nabiyyan wa adama bayna 'l-māʾi wa 't-tīn.
I was a Prophet when Adam was between soil and water.

Kuntu nabiyyan wa Adam bayn ar-rūh wa 'l-jasad.
I was a Prophet when Adam was between soul and body.

He was witnessing the soul and body of Sayyīdinā Adam ؑ.

ʿAn Jābir ibn ʿAbdAllāh bi-lafzh qāla: qultu ya Rasūlullāh, bi-abī anta wa ummī akhbarnī ʿana awwala shayin khalaqahu'Llāha qabla'l-ashyā? Qāla: ya Jābir, inn Allāha taʿala khalaqa qabla al-ashyā nūra nabiyyika min nūrih...

When Jābir ؓ asked, "Let my father and mother be sacrificed for you of Prophet of Allāh! What is the first thing that Allāh ﷻ created?" the Prophet ﷺ said, "The first thing that Allāh ﷻ created is the Light of your Prophet from His Light, O Jābir." (*Musannaf*, ʿAbdu 'r-Razzaq)

Imam Tirmidhi is saying that Allāh ﷻ created Sayyīdinā Muhammad ﷺ from the Light of the Essence with no intermediary. That is why Grandshaykh ق said that Allāh ﷻ first created the Light of the Prophet ﷺ. That is an explanation of the *ayah*:

اللَّهُ نُورُ السَّمَاوَاتِ وَالْأَرْضِ مَثَلُ نُورِهِ كَمِشْكَاةٍ فِيهَا مِصْبَاحٌ الْمِصْبَاحُ فِي زُجَاجَةٍ الزُّجَاجَةُ كَأَنَّهَا كَوْكَبٌ دُرِّيٌّ

Allāhu nūru 's-samāwāti wa 'l-ardi mathala nūrihi kamishkātin fīhā misbāh.

Allāh is the Light of the Heavens and Earth. The parable of His Light is as if there were a niche and within it a lamp. (Sūrat an-Nūr, 24:35)

That Light is Sayyīdinā Muḥammad ﷺ, *kawkabun durriyyun,* "a shining planet" or "brilliant star". Allāh ﷻ, with His Beautiful Names and Attributes—and He has not only Ninety-Nine Names, but Endless Names!—if we can say "looking", was looking at this Light in the Light for 70,000 years and in every moment of looking, Allāh ﷻ was dressing Sayyīdinā Muḥammad ﷺ with dresses that no one can understand and with Lights that come from the Divine Essence, *Dhāt al-Buht.*

And look at the eloquent description from Grandshaykh ق, from which you can visualize: "There is a Light and it is sweating from shyness of Allāh ﷻ, and that shyness produced heat inside that Lamp, on which there appeared heavenly condensation that we cannot describe, 124,000 drops, and from those drops Allāh created 124,000 prophets, and they were still in that Lamp. Then Allāh ﷻ was looking another 70,000 years and 124,000 more drops came and from these came the 124,000 *Ṣaḥābah.*"

And that number, 70,000 years, is very important in Shariʿah, as are the numbers "7007" and "70" and "7". For example, Allāh ﷻ said in Holy Qur'an that even if the Prophet ﷺ seeks forgiveness 70 times for the hypocrites, it will not be accepted, which makes that number very important! After those 124,000 prophets, Allāh ﷻ created 124,000 *awlīyā,* and then after that He created *Ummat an-Nabī* ﷺ and they number 400 billion.

Our realities are still inside that Lamp, they haven't come out, and that is why everyone here is a reflection of his original form! Here in *dunya* we have a reflection of our realities. That is why when some *awlīyāullāh* were born their eyes were open, not veiled, and for others their eyes were veiled and through their worship they progressed and those veils are removed. Grandshaykh ق said, "When I was born I was not veiled, but my eyes were always open and I was reading from the Preserved Tablet." This secret was passed to Mawlana Shaykh Nazim ق and he was dressed in it. So some *awlīyāullāh* have to progress through many levels for their eyes to open.

The Prophet ﷺ said that Allāh ﷻ said:

من عادا لي وليا فقد آذنته بالحرب

Man ʿadā lī waliyyan faqad ādhantahu bi 'l-harb.

Whoever comes against a wali of mine, I declare war on him!

(*Ḥadīth Qudsī*. Bukhari, from Abu Hurayrah)

ولا يزال عبدي يتقرب إلي بالنوافل حتى أحبه، فإذا أحببته كنت سمعه الذي يسمع به وبصره الذي يبصر به، ويده التي يبطش بها ورجله التي يمشي بها،

Wa lā yazāla ʿabdī yataqarabu ilayya bi' n-nawāfil hatta uhibbah. Fa idhā ahbābtahu kuntu samaʿuhulladhī yasmaʿu bihi wa basarahulladhī yubsiru bihi, wa yadahulladhī yabtishu bihā wa rijlahullatī yamshī bihā.

My servant does not cease to approach Me through voluntary worship until I will love him. When I love him, I will become the ears with which he hears, the eyes with which he sees, the hand with which he acts, and the legs with which he walks (and other versions include, "and the tongue with which he speaks.

(*Ḥadīth Qudsī*, Bukhari)

رب اشعث اغبر لو اقسم على الله لأبره

Rubba ashʿath aghbara law aqsama ʿala Allāhi lā-abbarah.

There may be a disheveled, dusty person who, if he swears an oath by Allāh, Allāh will fulfill it. (Muslim)

Allāh ﷻ looks at the hearts of people, not at their actions. So that is what we said yesterday, that anyone who makes one *ṣalawāt* on the Prophet ﷺ in the way Sayyīdinā ʿAlī ؓ narrated, Allāh ﷻ will give you the benefit of that *ṣalawāt* as if everyone from the day of Sayyīdinā Adam's Creation up to Judgment Day was reading *ṣalawāt* on the Prophet ﷺ, and all that is written for you! We were taught that *ṣalawāt* since I was nine years old and Shaykh Adnan was seven years old, because my father used to invite Shaykh Nazim to our home and we knew him since that time. He taught us that *ṣalawāt*.

Grandshaykh ʿAbdAllāh al-Faʿiz ad-Daghestani ق told us that *ṣalawāt* was written by Shaykh Sharafuddin ad-Daghestani ق and he gave it to us and to all *murīds*. He told us in seclusion he saw that if all human beings were standing in front of the Prophet ﷺ and reading *ṣalawāt*, standing any way they like, from beginning to end, if you read that *ṣalawāt* that Grandshaykh Sharafuddin ق recited, Allāh ﷻ will give them the rewards of all those people standing and doing *ṣalawāt* from the time of Sayyīdinā Adam ؑ to Judgment Day!

And we previously established that *awlīyāullāh* see the Prophet ﷺ in a dream or vision. Also, if you say to me, "The Prophet ﷺ came to me in a dream and said this and this," I have to say, "Yes," because of the *ḥadīth*, "Whoever saw me in a dream saw me in reality and will see me in the future, and Shayṭan cannot appear in my image."

I explained that Imam Bukhari never wrote a *ḥadīth* without first travelling from your country, China (and you know Quthum Ibn al-'Abbas ؓ is in your country, Uzbekistan), and he travelled one or two months to get one *ḥadīth* and before writing it he slept and would see the Prophet ﷺ saying to him if that *ḥadīth* is correct or not. So *awlīyāullāh* don't need to narrate the *isnad*, that this *ḥadīth* is from this one to that one, because they get directly from the Prophet ﷺ!

I was trying to find any source of that *du'a*, until I found not the whole *du'a* but part of it, in the book *Nahj al-Muttaqīn*, *Peak of the God-Fearing*, in which Sayyīdina 'Alī ؓ said if someone recites that *ṣalawāt* once, Allāh ﷻ will give them the benefit of all human beings having recited *ṣalawāt*! That *ṣalawāt* is:

> Ṣalawātullāhi wa malā'ikatihi wa anbiyāihi wa rusūlihi wa jami'ī khalqihi 'ala Muḥammad wa 'alā āli Muḥammad 'alayhi wa 'alayhimu 's-salām wa raḥmatullāhi wa barakatuh.

Both Imam Bukhari and Imam ibn Hajr al-Asqualani narrated that *ḥadīth*. Imam ibn Hajar said you also have to give *sadaqa*.

Holding One's Fingers in a Specific Way

We are not Buddhists, nor do we resemble Buddhists as some may think, because they say we join index finger and thumb, but all Muslims do that, especially in Turkey and Pakistan. Also, in some Muslims countries, when one hears *ṣalawāt* on the Prophet ﷺ, they kiss their thumb and forefinger and put them to their eyes and say, *qurrati 'ayna bika yā Sayyidī, yā Rasūlullāh*,

"My eyes are in happiness with you, O Master, O Rasūlullāh!" Even my uncle did that.

And why is it these particular fingers? Now science has come up with an explanation: the identity of a person is on the thumb and they say everything written about you is in it and it is made up of small points. That is your passport to Heaven or Hell.

This is the index finger, with which we make *shahādah,* bearing witness that there is no God but Allāh, and we put them together saying, "*Yā Rabbī*! With our heavenly ID/thumbprint, we witness that there is no god but Allāh and Muḥammad is His Messenger." Why do we put those same fingers on our eyes and say, *qurrati ʿaynī bika yā rasūlullāh,* "You are the coolness of my eyes, *yā Rasūlullāh*!" Now in England, when you enter the airport, to identify you they scan your iris, and from that scan every machine is notified about you. Similarly, every angel has been notified that you have witnessed that Allāh ﷻ is the Creator and Muḥammad ﷺ is His Prophet!

So with that we are not doing something outside of Islam, using the two fingers instead of one. As a reflection of one side to the other, we are using both hands. That is *ijtihad*.

Energy Points in the Human Body as Mentioned by Prophet

Everyone has a unique connection to Mawlana Shaykh Nazim that is different from the other, so if one got the knowledge and not the other that is okay, but you cannot exclude someone else's knowledge, such as knowledge of the 360 points! The Prophet ﷺ is the greatest and the best and he related *aḥadīth* in which he mentioned the miracle of points, recorded in *Saḥih Bukhari* and *Saḥih Muslim!*

I will say those who mentioned that *ḥadīth* are too many, but the last one is Sayyidatina ʿAyesha ؓ, and the Prophet ﷺ said, "Every one of Banī Adam are from 360 points or joints," because every joint is a point. When you go to a physical therapist, he presses on points. Why? He moves these joints in a certain way to relax you.

روى الإمام مسلم فى صحيحه قال:حدثنا حسن بن على الحلوانى. حدثنا أبو توبة الربيع بن نافع. حدثنا معاوية (يعنى ابن سلام) عن زيد ، أنه سمع أبا سلام يقول: حدثنى عبد الله بن فروخ ، أنه سمع عائشة تقول: إن رسول الله صلى الله عليه وسلم قال: " إنه خلق كل إنسان

من بنى آدم على ستين وثلاثمائة مفصل. فمن كبر الله، وحمد الله، وهلل الله، وسبح الله، واستغفر الله، وعزل حجرا عن طريق الناس، أو شوكة أو عظما من طريق الناس، وأمر بمعروف، أو نهى عن منكر، عدد تلك الستين والثلاثمائة السلامى. فإنه يمشى يومئذ وقد زحزح نفسه عن النار". قال أبو توبة: وربما قال"يمسى

The Prophet ﷺ said: Every one of the children of Adam has been created with 360 joints; so he who declares the Glory of Allāh, praises Allāh, declares Allāh to be One, Glorifies Allāh, and seeks forgiveness from Allāh, and removes an obstacle from people's path (like we have many obstacles in Cyprus blocking everyone), and enjoins what is good and forbids from evil, to the number of those 360 joints or points, will walk that Day toward Paradise, having removed himself from Hell. (Saḥih Muslim)

Wa man hallāhallāh wa sabaha Allāh...whoever makes *tahlīl, takbīr, tahmīd* and *istighfār* on the number of 360 points will walk as if he had saved himself from Hellfire! And he said, "Perhaps he will come at night and Allāh ﷻ will waive all his sins," because he made *tahlīl, takbīr, tahmīd, istighfar* 360 times. We can go more and more in depth in explaining that *ḥadīth*, as Imam Aḥmad said in his *Musnad*, "In the human beings there are 360 points and it is obligatory for him to give *ṣadaqah* on every joint/*mafsal*, then he will be okay."

روى الإمام أحمد فى مسنده قال: حَدَّثَنَا عَبْدُ اللَّهِ حَدَّثَنِى أَبِى حَدَّثَنَا زَيْدٌ حَدَّثَنِى حُسَيْنٌ حَدَّثَنِى عَبْدُ اللَّهِ بْنُ بُرَيْدَةَ قَالَ سَمِعْتُ أَبِى بُرَيْدَةَ يَقُولُ سَمِعْتُ رَسُولَ اللَّهِ -صلى الله عليه وسلم- يَقُولُ « فِى الإِنْسَانِ سِتُّونَ وَثَلاَثُمِائَةِ مَفْصِلٍ فَعَلَيْهِ أَنْ يَتَصَدَّقَ عَنْ كُلِّ مَفْصِلٍ مِنْهَا صَدَقَةً ». قَالُوا فَمَنِ الذي يُطِيقُ ذَلِكَ يَا رَسُولَ اللَّهِ قَالَ « النُّخَاعَةُ فِى الْمَسْجِدِ تَدْفِنُهَا أَوِ الشَّىْءُ تُنَحِّيهِ عَنِ الطَّرِيقِ فَإِنْ لَمْ تَقْدِرْ فَرَكْعَتَا الضُّحَى تُجْزِئُ عَنْكَ

I heard the Prophet say, "There are 360 joints (points) in the human body and for each joint you must give a ṣadaqah (thanks or charity) every day.

(Bukhari; Imam Aḥmad's *Musnad*)

Look how merciful the Prophet ﷺ is! When the *Ṣaḥābah* ﵃ said, *faman alladhī yudhi dhālika yā Rasūlullāh?* "Who can give that?" They were poor! And the Prophet ﷺ said, "If you cannot give *ṣadaqah,* then if you find dirtiness in the *masjid* and remove it, or you find something on the road that will harm someone and remove it, that will be considered *ṣadaqah.* And the *Ṣaḥābah* ﵃ asked for more guidance as they wanted some reduction, because they saw in the Last Days people are not going to do anything, that it might fall on one person to clean the *masjid*.

And the *ḥadīth* says if you pray two *raka'ats Ṣalāt ad-Duha* it will also suffice (to give *ṣadaqah* on those 360 points).

So why does anyone say that we take from Buddhists, why can't it be they are taking from us? Mawlana Shaykh is always saying there are five points in the heart: the *qalb, sirr, sirr o sirr, khafa* and *akhfa* points. Also, atoms are points and everything is from atoms, which means everything begins from a point! Fear Allāh ﷻ that He created everyone from one *nafs*, one point!

يَا أَيُّهَا النَّاسُ اتَّقُواْ رَبَّكُمُ الَّذِي خَلَقَكُم مِّن نَّفْسٍ وَاحِدَةٍ وَخَلَقَ مِنْهَا زَوْجَهَا وَبَثَّ مِنْهُمَا رِجَالاً كَثِيرًا وَنِسَاءوَاتَّقُواْ اللّهَ الَّذِي تَسَاءلُونَ بِهِ وَالأَرْحَامَ إِنَّ اللّهَ كَانَ عَلَيْكُمْ رَقِيبًا

Yā ayyuhā n-nāsu ittaqū rabbakumu 'Lladhī khalaqakum min nafsin wāhidatin wa khalaqa minhā zawjahā wa baththa minhumā rijālan kathīran wa nisān wa 't-aqū Allāha alladhī tasālūna bihi wa 'l-arhāma inna Allāha kāna 'alaykum raqība.

O mankind! Reverence your Guardian-Lord, Who created you from a single person, created of like nature his mate, and from them twain scattered (like seeds) countless men and women! Revere Allāh, through Whom you demand your mutual (rights), and (revere) the wombs (that bore you) for Allāh ever watches over you. (Sūrat an-Nisa, 4:1)

What is the beginning of every human being? A point: a sperm and an egg. Two points come together to make a human beings. How many sperms come? We have to say from science that every time 50-60 million sperms are released and they all go to one egg, although over time there are only 200 to 300 eggs.

And that is from the greatness of the Prophet ﷺ! But in the end you do find evidence, and I was surprised when our Egyptian brothers, who are very scientific, wanted to know what happened, how it is 360 points. So four doctors conducted research in a lab, three doctors of medicine and one doctor in Shari'ah. The Shari'ah manager was Dr. Mullāh al-Khatir. They read that *ḥadīth* and said it must be a miracle. So they decided to count the joints in a human being and here it is, so many pages long. I will not go through all of it, but will summarize. In vertebrae and hips there are 76 points. Do you know that? We don't know that, even medical doctors don't know that. They don't go deep into orthopedic science. When we were studying medicine we didn't count, we only looked at that skeleton. *Mafāsil al-Atrāf al-ʿUlwiyya, The Points of the Upper Body,* are 64 and the points of lower body are 62 and the total is 360, which is 360 points. Zoom the camera on this document[5] to see what the Prophet ﷺ spoke about. Who can do that?

Giving the Remainder of Your Life to Extend Another's

We will begin discussion of this topic by first looking at evidence from *aḥadīth*:

وفي موته يروي الترمذي: عن أبي هريرة قال: قال رسول الله صلى الله عليه وسلم : "لما خلق الله آدم مسح ظهره، فسقط من ظهره كل نسمة هو خالقها من ذريته إلى يوم القيامة، وجعل بين عيني كل إنسان منهم وبيصاً من نور، ثم عرضهم على آدم فقال: أي رب من هؤلاء؟ قال: هؤلاء ذريتك، فرأى رجلاً فأعجبه وبيص ما بين عينيه، فقال: أي رب من هذا؟ قال هذا رجل من آخر الأمم من ذريتك يقال له داود، قال: رب وكم جعلت عمره؟ قال ستين سنة، قال: أي رب زده من عمري أربعين سنة. فلما انقضى عمر آدم جاءه ملك الموت، قال: أو لم يبق من عمري أربعون سنة؟ قال: أو لم تعطها ابنك داود؟ قال فجحد فجحدت ذريته، ونسي آدم فنسيت ذريته، وخطىء آدم فخطئت ذريته"

> *Lama khalaqa Allāhu adam massaha zhahra. Fasaqata min zhahrihi kullu nasamatin huwa khāliquhā min zhurriyatahu ila yawm al-qiyāmat. Wa jʿala bayna ʿaynay kullu insānin minhum wabīsan min nūr. Thumma ʿaradahum ʿala adam faqāla: ayy Rabb, man hāūlā'i? Qāla: hā'ūlā'i dhuriyyatik. Fa-ra'a rajulan fa-ʿajabahu wabīsa mā bayna ʿaynayh. Faqāla: ayy Rabb, man hadhā? Qāla rajulun min ākhir al-umami min dhurriyatik yuqāla lahu dāwūd. Qāla: rabbi wa kam jaʿalta ʿumrihi? Qāla: sittīna sannah. Qāla: ayy Rabb zidhu min ʿumrī arbaʿīn sannah. Falamā anqada ʿamra adam ja'ahu malak al-mawt. Qāl: awa lam yabiq min ʿumrī arbaʿīna sannah? Qāla: awa lam tuʿtahā 'bnuka dawūd? Qāla fajahada fajahadta dhurriyatah wa nasiya fa nasiya dhurriyatah. Wa khatā adam fa-khata'at dhurriyatah.*

[5] You can see this document with researchers' names and total points in the body online at http://tl.gd/gk2o61.

Abu Hurayrah ﷺ has narrated that the Prophet ﷺ said: "When Allāh created Adam, He stroked with His Hand over his back. So all the souls which were due to be born in his progeny until the Day of Judgment, came out of his back. In front of the eyes of every human He made a shining light and placed them all before Adam. Adam said: "O Lord! Who are they?" He replied, "They are your progeny." He saw a man among them whose shining light attracted him. Adam asked: "O Lord! Who is this?" Allāh answered him, "He is a man who will come in the last of your progeny, and who will be called Dawūd." He asked Him, "O Lord! How much have You granted him of his age?" Allāh said, "Sixty years." Adam asked Allāh, "O Lord! Grant him from my age forty years more." When the Angel of Death came to take his soul he said, "Does not there remain from my lifespan forty years?" The Angel of Death said, "Did you not give over forty of your years to Dawūd?" He said, "He denied, and his descendants denied after him and he forgot and his descendants forgot after him and he made the mistake and his descendants made mistakes."

(*Ḥasan ḥadīth* related in *Saḥih at-Tirmidhi*)

Every *nasma,* all that Allāh ﷻ is going to create of all Creation, dripped from his back. I am going to bring from that *ḥadīth* the reason why human beings are called *"insān,"* which comes from the word, "forgetfulness," and we forget everything, good or bad, which is a mercy from Allāh ﷻ to human beings that they keep forgetting, "I did this bad and this bad." And if they remember goodness they are going to be proud, "I did this and I did that!" So Allāh made *insān* to forget.

When Allāh ﷻ stroked the back of Sayyīdinā Adam ﷺ, all his offspring came out and He made between the eyes of every human being a ray of Light coming out, *wabīsan min nūr*, and that is the Light of Muḥammad ﷺ:

وإعلموا أن فيكم رسول الله

W'alamū anna fīkum rasūlullāh.

And know Allāh's Messenger is in you. (Sūrat al-Ḥujurāt, 49:7)

The Light of Rasūlullāh is in you! It is not what they write in English translations, "the Prophet ﷺ is between you", which would be *"baynakum"* or *"ma'akum"*, but here it is "in you"! So he saw that Light coming and in each one the Light is different, and then He showed these to Sayyīdinā Adam ﵇, as indicated in the verse:

وَعَلَّمَ آدَمَ الأَسْمَاء كُلَّهَا

Wa ʿallama adama al-asmā kullāhā.

He taught Adam all the names. (Sūrat al-Baqarah, 2:31)

We will not go into that *tafsīr* now; there might be Names of Allāh ﷻ or of the Prophet ﷺ, or names Allāh ﷻ gave him, but he said he saw these Lights coming from them. And then Adam ﵇ saw one man among them whose Light he liked so much! And we said that was the Light of Sayyīdinā Muḥammad ﷺ, and that the reason *Iblīs* refused to make *sajdah* to Sayyīdinā Adam ﵇ was because the Light of Sayyīdinā Muḥammad ﷺ was in the forehead of Sayyīdinā Adam ﵇. He said to Allāh ﷻ, *"You created me from fire and You created him from mud!"* He was arrogant, so we have to leave arrogance and we have to like that Light.

So he said, "Who is that one?" And Allāh ﷻ said, "That is a man from the last nations, from your offspring." Then he asked, "O my Lord! How many years did you make his life?" Allāh ﷻ said, "I made his life sixty years." Sayyīdinā Adam ﵇ said, "O my Lord! Increase his life from my life by forty years. I accept to give forty years from my life to him." After some time, the Angel of Death came to him and he said, "What are you coming to do?" The Angel of Death ﵇ said, "I am coming to take your soul." "How are you coming now? It is not time to give it yet!" The Angel of Death said, "Did you not give it to your son, Dawūd?" But Sayyīdinā Adam ﵇ had forgotten that he gave his forty years to Dawūd ﵇!

So you gave it and now forgot it, and so now Sayyīdinā Adam ﵇ didn't like it! Many people might say to the Prophet ﷺ, "I give the life of my father and mother and myself!" and sometimes Allāh accepted it from them so they died! And Sayyīdinā Adam ﵇ did hate that. That means he made a sin now! And also his offspring cannot give their soul, it is very difficult, but some might give their life to the Prophet ﷺ to *awlīyāullāh* and many might give their life. And many of you I am sure will say, if their child is sick, "O Allāh! Take from my life and give to my child!" so Allāh ﷻ may accept and take from your life and give to the other.

We will continue next time with accounts of Sayyīdinā Muḥammad Zahid al-Bukhari ☬, Sayyīdinā 'Ubaydullāh al-Aḥrar ق, and Mawlana Qassim ق regarding this issue and explaining that *ḥadīth*.

I am not criticizing anyone here, I am only explaining to or educating myself, and if anyone of you want to listen it is up to you. We are only mentioning *aḥadīth* and the Holy Qur'an. Also, we must not forget things that we do; we must not be arrogant and we must ask pardon from those we harmed, for the sake of the Prophet ﷺ and for the sake of Mawlana Shaykh, that Allāh ﷻ will take away from us the *fitna* of this *dunya* and remove from us *ghība* and *namīma*, backbiting and slander, to be clean in front of Mawlana Shaykh Nazim ق in this life and the Next.

May Allāh ﷻ forgive us and may Allāh ﷻ bless us.

Wa min Allāhi 't-tawfīq, bi ḥurmati 'l-ḥabīb, bi ḥurmati 'l-Fātiḥah.

And with Allāh is success. For the sake of the Beloved, for his sake we recite the opening chapter of Holy Qur'an.

The All-Encompassing Power of the Purest Love

A'ūdhu billāhi min ash-Shayṭāni 'r-rajīm. Bismillāhi' r-Raḥmāni 'r-Raḥīm.
Nawaytu 'l-arbā'īn, nawaytu 'l-'itikāf, nawaytu'l-khalwah, nawaytu 'l-'uzlah,
nawaytu 'r-riyāḍa, nawaytu 's-sulūk, lillāhi Ta'alā fī hādhā 'l-masjid.
Atī'ūllāha wa atī'ū 'r-Rasūla wa ūlī 'l-amri minkum.
Obey Allāh, obey the Prophet, and obey those in authority among you. (4:59)

Dastūr, madad yā Sulṭān al-Awlīyā, Mawlana Shaykh Nazim al-Haqqani ق.
Dastūr, madad yā Sulṭān al-Awlīyā, Mawlana Shaykh 'AbdAllāh ad-Daghestani ق.

They say every *ṣalāt* with *miswāk* equals twenty-seven *ṣalāt* without *miswāk*. The *adab* of using the *miswak* is to sit like this (on knees, covering the mouth) and to recite, *Allāhumma ṭāhhir qalbī min ash-shirki wa 'n-nifāq*, "O Allāh! Purify my heart of idolatry and hypocrisy." When the enemy was approaching, the Prophet ﷺ told the Ṣaḥābah ؓ to go on their knees and rub their teeth with the *miswāk*, and as soon as they did that the enemy ran away, thinking the Ṣaḥābah ؓ were going to eat them! The *tajallī* of using the *siwāk* is to scare Shayṭan, and by using *siwāk* your prayer is 27 times better.

We spoke of the Greatness of the Prophet ﷺ and of how the one who loves the Prophet ﷺ will move and speak in his ﷺ presence, keeping *adab*. Allāh ﷻ said in Holy Qur'an:

يُحِبُّهُمْ وَيُحِبُّونَهُ

Yuhibbuhum wa yuhibbūnahum.
People whom He loves and who love Him.   (Sūrat al-Ma'idah, 5:54)

He loves them and they love him! I will tell you one incident that took place after Friday prayers in Damascus. Grandshaykh ق used to give *ṣuḥbah* after *Jumu'ah* and lead *dhikr*, which did not exceed thirty minutes. Usually he sat on a cushion in an area twice as big as this *masjid*. Some people sat on cushions and some sat in rows on the floor. My brother Shaykh Adnan and I usually sat directly facing Grandshaykh ق, and Mawlana Shaykh Nazim ق was on his right translating. One time, my brother and I thought, "Why is Mawlana sitting on cushions? Let us make nicer cushions for him," as Baba

Tahseen, may Allāh bless his soul, made nice cushions for Mawlana Shaykh Nazim ق. So we made nice cushions and Grandshaykh ق saw them and sat on them and prayed for those who made that sweet, nice gesture. We didn't say anything and Mawlana didn't say anything. That was in 1968.

In 1973, four months before Grandshaykh ق had his operation and left *dunya,* he was sick and lying in bed, but we know that he was not really sick. Then he wanted to show who is the one to be respected after him, to give us a sign. Every *wali* gives that sign, as the Prophet ﷺ did with Sayyīdinā Abu Bakr as-Siddiq ؓ when he was sick and he ordered Abu Bakr to lead the prayers and he closed all windows of the houses of the *Ṣaḥābah* ؓ, except the window of Abu Bakr as-Siddiq, which is still open up to today.

As I said previously, the letter *"Hā"* in the word *"hubb,"* love, stands for *"hayāt,"* life, and the *"Bā"* stands for *"baqa',"* eternal existence. So when a person loves someone, from their intense love the remembrance of that someone always exists in his mind and heart. Similarly, the love of the shaykh stays there eternally, it never goes! On the other hand, the shaykh's love to his *murīds* stays with him and he will not enter Paradise without taking them with him to Eternal Life, as the Prophet ﷺ will not enter Paradise without taking whole *ummah,* and there are many *aḥadīth* on this subject.

So Mawlana Shaykh Nazim ق was very happy with that gesture of the new cushions. He didn't say anything, but he prayed, "Those who love me, may Allāh ﷻ love them!" as Allāh ﷻ said:

قُلْ إِن كُنتُمْ تُحِبُّونَ اللَّهَ فَاتَّبِعُونِي يُحْبِبْكُمُ اللَّهُ وَيَغْفِرْ لَكُمْ ذُنُوبَكُمْ وَاللَّهُ غَفُورٌ رَّحِيمٌ

Qul in kuntum tuhibbūna 'Llāha fattabiʿūnī yuhbibkumullāhu wa yaghfir lakum dhunūbakum w 'Allāhu Ghafūru 'r-Rahīm.

Say (O Muḥammad), "If you (really) love Allāh, then follow me! Allāh will love you and forgive your sins, and Allāh is Oft-Forgiving, Most Merciful.

(Sūrat Āli-'Imrān, 3:31)

You have to love Allāh ﷻ and the Prophet ﷺ more than you love yourself, as the Prophet ﷺ said:

لا يؤمن أحدكم حتى أكون أحب إليه من ولده ووالده والناس أجمعين. وفي رواية ومن نفسه التي بين جنبيه

La yu'minū ahadukum hatta akūna ahabba ilayhi min waladihi wa walidihi wa 'n-nāsī ajmaʿīn. wa fi riwāya wa min nafsi 'l-ladhī bayna jambayhi.

You are not considered a believer until you love me more than you love your son, your father, and all of humanity.[6] (Bukhari)

The Prophet ﷺ is saying, "None of you is considered a believer until he loves me more than all his family." That is why Allāh ﷻ gives to *awlīyāullāh,* because they leave even their families for the sake of the Prophet ﷺ! If you tell me that Mawlana Shaykh Nazim ق didn't leave his family, clearly you have no knowledge of him! He often left his family to travel for Grandshaykh ق, entering seclusion for forty days, six months, nine months, one year, and also traveling all around, not waiting in one place for people to come to him.

After his seclusion in *Madinatu 'l-Munawwara* in 1969, Grandshaykh ق said, "When I was returning to Sham, the Prophet ﷺ said to me, *'Yā Waladī*! Don't run after people; rather, people will come to you. I am sending *mukhlisī ummatī,* the most sincere of my *ummah* to you!'" I remember this as if I am seeing it now. Mawlana Shaykh Nazim ق is carrying that secret, because the next shaykh carries whatever secret his shaykh has that was given from Prophet ﷺ.

So that is why we see Mawlana Shaykh Nazim ق is like a spotlight, a magnet to whom people from east and west are drawn. Many people contact us through the Internet and although they don't know Mawlana Shaykh Nazim, from only reading his *suḥbahs* they want to see him and they are coming. And it is not simple to come, to pay US $2,000-$3,000 to see the shaykh, and even you might not even see him! That shows that everyone who comes here is a sincere person who will be under the *shafaʿā* of the Prophet ﷺ! We cannot say 'under the wings', but they are under the protection of Mawlana Shaykh Muḥammad Nazim al-Haqqani ق, Grandshaykh ʿAbdAllāh al-Faʿiz ad-Daghestani ق, Shaykh Sharafuddin ad-

[6] And in another narration, *"... and love me more than yourself."*

Daghestani ق and Shaykh Abu Aḥmad as-Sughuri ق, all the way back to the Prophet ﷺ!

Before I mention about the chair we made for Mawlana Shaykh, I would like to read the *ḥadīth* they just sent me. Everyone here believes whatever I say, but there are some people on the Internet that might not, because they are square-headed people who, regarding everything we say, constantly ask, "Where is your evidence?"

Imam Shafiʿī ؓ said, "If one-hundred scholars come to question me I will win, but if one *jāhil,* ignorant comes to me, he will win." Ignorant ones always question, "Where is your proof? Show us the evidence."

Numbers in Islam

Grandshaykh ق said that *Ummat an-Nabī* ﷺ will consist of 400 billion people on Judgment Day, and I also heard it from Mawlana Shaykh Nazim ق. Like the *ṣalawāt* of Grandshaykh Sharafuddin ad-Daghestani ق that we recently mentioned, I never found it anywhere until I recently found that part of it was related by Sayyīdinā ʿAlī ؓ, in the book *Nahj al-Muttaqīn, Peak of the God-Fearing*. Grandshaykh ق said whoever recites that *ṣalawāt* one time will receive the reward of all human beings from the time of Sayyīdinā Adam ؑ to Judgment Day, reciting it while standing!

As for the *ummah* of the Prophet ﷺ being 400 billion people, I didn't find any text on it until recently. Grandshaykh ق used to tell us to pick up a book, which is to show helplessness and weakness when we deliver *suḥbahs,* and he cautioned us not to say things from east to west that people like to hear but from which they may not understand anything. It is not imaginings, like those who casually speak of the Divine Essence, *Dhāt al-Buht*, where people don't understand such deep topics. So you have to be careful.

When I was young, I often wondered where I could find this, and recently I did. Imam Ghazali ؓ mentioned towards the end of his book *Faysal at-Tafriqa, The Boundaries of Religious Tolerance in Islam,* "The Prophet ﷺ will intercede for the *ummah* 70,000 times 70,000 times 70,000." Just like we read in *Dalāʾil al-Khayrāt*, "*Allāhumma salli ʿala Sayyīdinā Muḥammad alfa alfa marrah,*" "*alfa alfa*" is one million, "*alfa alfa alfa*" is one billion, and "*alfa alfa alfa alfa*" is beyond what we can count, and 70,000 times 70,000 times

70,000 is 343 billion people, very near 400 billion, which is what Grandshaykh said is the number of human beings in the *ummah* of Sayyīdinā Muḥammad ﷺ.

The scholar Mustafa ar-Rafiʿī suggested on page 68 of his book, *'Ijāz al-Qurʿan, The Miraculous Nature of the Qur'an,* "The number seven has the symbolic meaning of perfection," and the Prophet ﷺ mainly used the numbers seven and zero. In numerology, zero represents nothing; it is annihilation, that nothing exists except Allāh, while the number seven represents the Seven Paradises that Allāh ﷻ will give everyone on the Day of Judgment. So that shows us that when *awlīyāullāh* say something, if you didn't understand it don't object, but rather say, "They know better."

Familiarity Extinguishes Good Manners

Everyone loves the shaykh and so they move according to the love in their heart and sometimes that makes conflict and sometimes it goes easy, because it is not possible that everyone has the same level, just as everyone's fingerprints and irises are different. Therefore, you might like this one and he might like that one; you might like this shaykh and he likes another shaykh. *Alḥamdulillāh* we are guided to *Sulṭān al-Awlīyā,* Mawlana Shaykh Nazim al-Haqqani ق, but that doesn't mean other *murīds* don't love their shaykh.

So coming back to the story, when we put the cushions Grandshaykh ق was in his room and he told Mawlana Shaykh Nazim ق, "Go do the *dhikr.*" Mawlana Shaykh went up the steps slowly and Grandshaykh said, *billāhi ʿalayk,* "Don't reject by Allāh," meaning, "Go and do the *dhikr* as I cannot, I have no energy." So Mawlana Shaykh Nazim went up, and we love him so we arranged the cushions before he came, fluffing and putting them back nicely, and Mawlana looked at it and read Fātiḥah, and he sat like Shaykh Bahauddin is sitting now, not on the chair.

We said, "Mawlana please sit here," but he said, "No. I am afraid because to be near the Sultan is to be near fire. Any mistake or any unacceptable move can put you in a problem. And Shaykh ʿAbdAllāh didn't say, 'Sit in my chair.' *Adaban* is to behave as if he is sitting now, present here, so I have to sit on the side," and he sat on the side.

Let us mention another story from which we will benefit. Grandshaykh had five representatives: Mawlana Shaykh Nazim, Shaykh Husayn, Abu Muḥammad al-Miʿdāmi, Shaykh Abu ʿEsam and Shaykh Farouq. After that incident happened with the chair, we were sitting and Grandshaykh's place was empty, although he was spiritually present on his chair except for his soul. Someone came from the door all the way and sat in Grandshaykh's place, and took his *miswāk* and hit Mawlana Shaykh Nazim on the head, and Shaykh Nazim did not say one word! That person said, "This is not your place, this is my place! I'm a representative (superior to you)!" If a representative of Grandshaykh ʿAbdAllāh acted like that, what behavior do you expect from some representatives today?

And then the story continues, but I will not narrate it here except to say that they escorted him out as if nothing happened. If that happened to any other representative, they would feel humiliated. So we learned from Mawlana Shaykh Nazim ق that the proper *adab* is to not sit where the shaykh sits, or to use the same plate he uses, etc., so as not to make yourself familiar with him, because familiarity is only for the shaykh's family and *murīds* must know their boundaries.

We used to enter Grandshaykh's house freely, then one day he said to us, "O my son! Don't look at how I interact with my family as I must treat them as normal human beings, but *murīds* must be very careful as that does not apply to them. They must be very respectful, know their boundaries and not transgress their limits or they might be in a problem without even knowing it!" After that we were very careful, but undoubtedly he loved us very much. For many years, we came to Damascus from Beirut at two o'clock in the morning and knocked on Mawlana Shaykh Nazim's door, made *wudu* with him, then went to Grandshaykh ʿAbdAllāh's house and prayed all the way up to *Fajr* and *Ishrāq*, then returned to Beirut.

Of course we are not saying that you may not love your shaykh, no. In fact, one must become annihilated with the shaykh, giving their life to him, to achieve the states of *Fanā'un fī 'Llāh, Fanā'un fī 'l-Habīb, Fanā'un fī 'sh-Shaykh*, Annihilation in Allāh, Annihilation in The Beloved, Annihilation in the shaykh.

In 1940, before we knew him, Mawlana Shaykh Nazim ق left Cyprus completely, although they were a very wealthy family that owned land and homes in Nicosia. Grandshaykh ق told us that Mawlana Shaykh Nazim ق

sold everything and gave all his money to Grandshaykh ق without leaving a penny. He said to us, "Look at how big his love is; he gave all that he had." Grandshaykh ق used that money to buy two parcels of land in Harasta and Douma. Mawlana Shaykh Nazim ق didn't even look back after giving everything to Grandshaykh ق, and when he made his will, Grandshaykh ق distributed that land among his family, and Mawlana Shaykh didn't say anything. So indeed, people love the shaykh, but there must be boundaries. The Ṣaḥābah ؎ loved Prophet Muḥammad ﷺ; also, Sayyīdinā Abu Bakr ؎ gave everything in the way of Allāh ﷻ. We do not doubt anyone's love to the shaykh, as everyone loves according to his level.

يحشر المرء مع من أحب

Yuhshar al-maruw maʿ man ahab.
The Prophet ﷺ said: Each person will be resurrected with the one he loves.

You will be resurrected with the one you love the most. If you love your shaykh the most, you will be resurrected with your shaykh; if you love your wife the most, you will be resurrected with your wife; or, if you love your children the most and they are on the right way, you will be resurrected with them. You will also be under the intercession of Prophet ﷺ.

I will relate a story coming from the chain that links to Sayyīdinā Muḥammad ﷺ, who is the main source. It is related by Muḥammad Zahid ق, who came after Shaykh ʿUbaydullāh al-Aḥrar ق, who is buried in a cemetery in Samarqand reserved exclusively for scholars. This story is about one of his *murīds*, Muḥammad Qassim ق. One time Shaykh ʿUbaydullāh al-Aḥrar ق was very sick, so he ordered his *murīd*, Muḥammad Zahid, to go to Herat, Iran and bring a doctor, which happened because the shaykh saw something that was hidden from others and he wanted to expose it. Just as on the Day of Promises when Sayyīdinā Adam ؏ was shown his descendants, he prayed to Allāh ﷻ to give forty years of his life to Sayyīdinā Dawud ؏, and Allāh ﷻ accepted his *duʿa*.

So Mawlana Qassim ق told Muḥammad Zahid, "Go quickly because I cannot stand to see my shaykh sick!" What happened when the Prophet ﷺ passed away? Sayyīdinā ʿUmar ؎ said, "Whoever says Muḥammad ﷺ died, I will kill him!" and Sayyīdinā Abu Bakr as-Siddiq ؎ said, "Yā ʿUmar, don't say that," and then recited the following verse from the Holy Qurʾan:

وَمَا مُحَمَّدٌ إِلاَّ رَسُولٌ قَدْ خَلَتْ مِن قَبْلِهِ الرُّسُلُ أَفَإِن مَّاتَ أَوْ قُتِلَ انقَلَبْتُمْ عَلَى أَعْقَابِكُمْ وَمَن يَنقَلِبْ عَلَىَ عَقِبَيْهِ فَلَن يَضُرَّ اللّهَ شَيْئًا وَسَيَجْزِي اللّهُ الشَّاكِرِينَ

Wa mā Muḥammadun illā rasūlun qad khalat min qablihi 'r-rasūlu afa'in māta aw qutila inqalabtum 'alā 'aqābikum wa man yanqalib 'alā 'aqibayhi falan yadurra 'Llāha shayan wa sayajzī 'Llāhu 'sh-shākirīn.

Muḥammad is no more than a messenger; many messengers passed away before him. If he died or were slain, will you then turn back on your heels (as disbelievers)? And he who turns back on his heels, not the least harm will he do to Allāh, and Allāh will reward to those who are grateful.

(Sūrat Āli 'Imrān, 3:144)

Then Sayyīdinā 'Umar ؓ said, "*Yā* Abu Bakr! It is as if I never heard that verse before."

Mawlana Qassim ق urged him to go quickly. Muḥammad Zahid ق said, "I left in such a hurry that I didn't even go home, but went straight to my destination. It took me thirty-five days to get the doctor. When I came back, I learned that shaykh 'Ubaydullāh al-Aḥrar ق was completely cured and the *murīd*, Mawlana Qassim ق had passed away although he was very strong physically and a wrestler and very good sportsman of archery and fencing. For this reason, I was surprised and wished to inquire about this incident, so I asked Shaykh 'Ubaydullāh al-Aḥrar ق about this.

He answered, 'Muḥammad Qassim came to me one day and said, 'I sacrifice myself to you,'" like how the *Ṣaḥābah* ؓ came to the Prophet ﷺ and said, "We give our life to you!" Because he knew if a *ṣādiq murīd* with real *hubb* asks Allāh ﷻ for something, Allāh ﷻ will accept. "I said to him, 'Don't say that another time; you have people whom you gather and look after. You take their hands.'" But no way Muḥammad Qassim could not do that, because when the love is intense, even if the shaykh tells him not to do that, the *murīd* will not accept his advice. "He said to me, 'O my shaykh! I am not asking you nor did I come to consult with you on this matter, but in fact I decided this within myself and it is finished. I came to you inform you that Allāh has accepted my request.'" This *murīd* was also a *walī*. Shaykh 'Ubaydullāh ق said, "I repeatedly told him not to do that, but he insisted and did not change his mind." So the next day, the illness of the shaykh transferred to Mawlana Qassim and he experienced shortness of breath and passed away, while the shaykh became completely cured and was no longer in need of the doctor."

I was completely amazed by this story as it goes beyond the mind! When love is true you cannot think, as that state takes one beyond all boundaries of the mind. I gave *dalīl* yesterday from the *ḥadīth* of the Prophet ﷺ and now from the book *Al-Hadāiq al-Wardiyya Fī Ṭarīqat an-Naqshbandi.* This story is further related in *Rashahat ʿAyn al-Hayat,* a similar book on The Naqshbandi Order:

> Without any protest or argument, Qassim left ʿUbaydullāh al-Aḥrar and died shortly after having taken the venerable Khawaja's illness upon himself. The venerable Khawaja recovered his health and got up from his bed. The physician who had come was no longer needed. While Mawlana Qassim was at the point of death, ʿUbaydullāh al-Aḥrar ق stood at his bedside.

The shaykh can stand near any person, physically or spiritually; it has happened to me. Once I was between life and death, and Mawlana Shaykh Nazim was at my bedside.

> Mawlana Qassim lay motionless with his eyes glued at a spot on the ceiling. He suddenly turned his gaze to the venerable Khawaja and took his last breath in that position and died. Sayyīdinā ʿUbaydullāh al-Aḥrar said, "Why do you think he was looking at that corner on the ceiling and then to me? Because all the Gardens of Paradise with all their richness, glamor, happiness, *hūr al-ʿayn* and *wildan,* were displayed to Mawlana Qassim at that spot. He had his eyes fixed there, but he preferred to turn his face away from it all. Although it is the best, he turned his face to look at us instead and thus, he died looking at me. I was by his bed."

Think to yourself, how much love a *murīd* or a representative can have towards his shaykh? Where are we and where are they? We are very low, helpless, and *mashā-Allāh* they are very high. Our *shuyūkh* are not as we see them, they are as they see us!

Prophet ﷺ said:

شفاعتي لأهل الكبائر من أمتي

Shafaʿtī li ahl al-kabāʾir min ummatī.

My intercession is for big sinners on Judgment Day. (Imam Aḥmad)

I discussed this with Mawlana Shaykh Nazim ق, that daily people are making millions of *ṣalawāt* on the Prophet ﷺ, but on the Day of Judgment new prayers will be opened to Prophet ﷺ that were never opened before, as related in the book *Adab al-Mufrad* of Imam Bukhari:

> The Prophet ﷺ will go into *sajda* on the Day of Judgment, and Allāh ﷻ will open *duʿas* to him that were never opened to him before. Allāh ﷻ will then tell him to raise his head and ask, and Prophet ﷺ will raise his head and hands and ask for his *ummah.* Allāh ﷻ will say, "Go and take one-third of them." The Prophet ﷺ will not be satisfied; he will go into *sajda* once more and make prayers that were never opened before. Then again Allāh ﷻ will say, "Ask and you will be given." Prophet ﷺ will ask for his *ummah* and Allāh ﷻ will give him another third of the *ummah.* Then the Prophet ﷺ will go into *sajda* and new prayers will be opened to him that were never opened before. Allāh ﷻ will tell him to raise his head and ask. Prophet ﷺ will raise his head and hands and ask for his *ummah.* Allāh ﷻ will then say, "Take all of them, except for that one!" That person will be the worst of the entire *ummah*, and everyone must think it may be them, as we are all sinners from the Prophet's ﷺ nation. Then Allāh will ask, "Who gave My Mercy to Muḥammad ﷺ? I did, as I am *Arḥama 'r-Raḥimīn*! I am The Best, *Raḥmah* on *Raḥmah!* Go with Prophet ﷺ to Paradise without *hisāb,* giving any account!"

This is what Prophet ﷺ said, and therefore, we cannot deny it! So *yā Rasūlullāh*! We are expecting from you because we love you, we love our shaykh, we love our Way! Without looking at our bad *ʿamal,* with your intercession take us to Paradise!

May Allāh ﷻ forgive us and may Allāh ﷻ bless us.

Wa min Allāhi 't-tawfiq, bi ḥurmati 'l-ḥabīb, bi ḥurmati 'l-Fātiḥah.

And with Allāh is success. For the sake of the Beloved, for his sake we recite the opening chapter of Holy Qur'an.

Saved from Punishment of the Grave

Aʿūdhu billāhi min ash-Shayṭāni 'r-rajīm. Bismillāhi' r-Raḥmāni 'r-Raḥīm.
Nawaytu 'l-arbāʿīn, nawaytu 'l-ʿitikāf, nawaytu'l-khalwah, nawaytu 'l-ʿuzlah,
nawaytu 'r-riyāḍa, nawaytu 's-sulūk, lillāhi Taʿalā fī hādhā 'l-masjid.
Atīʿūllāha wa atīʿū 'r-Rasūla wa ūlī 'l-amri minkum.
Obey Allāh, obey the Prophet, and obey those in authority among you. (4:59)

Dastūr, madad yā Sulṭān al-Awlīyā, Mawlana Shaykh Nazim al-Haqqani ق.
Dastūr, madad yā Sulṭān al-Awlīyā, Mawlana Shaykh ʿAbdAllāh ad-Daghestani ق.

We are speaking about the Greatness of Prophet ﷺ. I recently heard Mawlana Shaykh Nazim ق say that he wants to open a school in Famagusta, Cyprus to teach the Greatness of Prophet ﷺ, with the intention that students not only memorize Holy Qur'an and *ḥadīth,* but also to make people aware of the Greatness of Sayyīdinā Muḥammad ﷺ, because too many today are not giving importance to that subject.

Throughout history you find how much scholars and common people of previous times respected Prophet ﷺ. You see whenever Mawlana Shaykh Nazim ق mentions the name of Prophet ﷺ, he puts his hand over his chest to invoke peacefulness or tranquility in his heart, or he stands up to give *tʿazhīmu 'n-Nabī,* grandeur to Prophet ﷺ!

There have been many scholars among *Ahlu 's-Sunnah wa 'l-Jamaʿah,* by whom I mean the people who accept *tasawwuf,* and most of them accept *tasawwuf* up to today. The right name for them is "*Ahlu 's-Sunnah wa'l-Jamaʿah,*" and now other groups use that name although they consider Prophet ﷺ to be only a man who came and is now gone! Without mentioning their names, we know their names already and they pretend they are *Ahlu 's-Sunnah wa 'l-Jamaʿah,* but the authentic *Ahlu 's-Sunnah wa 'l-Jamaʿah* are those who love Prophet ﷺ more than their parents, themselves and their children!

We will mention some stories and *aḥadīth* of Prophet ﷺ from the book *Manahij as-Saʿadāt, The Ways of Happiness.*

Akthirū min as-ṣalāti ʿalayya yawmu 'l-jumuʿati wa laylatu 'l-jumuʿah.

Try to be excessive in prayers on me on the day and night of Friday.

(Imam Shafiʿī in his *Musnad*; Ibn Habbān; Ibn Majah; Abu Dawūd)

It means do as much *ṣalawāt* as possible and don't sit around being lazy! Why must we do it? We can recite *ṣalawāt* ten times, a hundred times, and some people a thousand times, but why so many; why do you have to do one-million times, two-million times? The square-headed people whose names we don't want to mention say if you do too much *ṣalawāt,* you are committing *shirk*! We ask, did Allāh ﷻ make *shirk* when He ordered His angels to make *ṣalawāt* on the Prophet ﷺ?

Allāh ﷻ said:

إِنَّ اللَّهَ وَمَلَائِكَتَهُ يُصَلُّونَ عَلَى النَّبِيِّ يَا أَيُّهَا الَّذِينَ آمَنُوا صَلُّوا عَلَيْهِ وَسَلِّمُوا تَسْلِيمًا

Inna-Llāha wa malā'ikatahu yusallūna ʿala 'n-nabiyy, yā ayyuhal-ladhīna āmanū sallū ʿalayhi was sallimū taslīma.

Verily, Allāh and His angels send praise on the Prophet. O Believers! Pray upon him and greet him. (Sūrat al-'Aḥzāb, 33:56)

The word "*yusallūna*" is not past tense or present tense, it is the future tense. Which comes first? Past tense, *faʿl al-mādiyy,* and then present tense, *faʿl al-ḥāḍir,* then future tense, *faʿl al-mustaqbal.* Why does past come first, then present, then future? Because the past was the future, then became present, then became past. I "am opening" a book is present tense; I "opened" the book is past tense; I "will open" the book is future tense. But in religion there is no past, present or future, everything is in the present, as the present moment is what matters. So what is Allāh saying? "Allāh and His angels are praising and praying on the Prophet," in the future tense, which means they are continuously making *ṣalawāt* on the Prophet ﷺ.

A question comes here: did Allāh ﷻ say to the angels, *"inna Allāh salla ʿalā an-Nabī mi'at marrah,"* pray on the Prophet ﷺ a hundred times, or did He order His angels to pray a hundred times on the Prophet ﷺ? No, He and His angels are continuously praising the Prophet ﷺ, and then it is an order for all humanity, *"yā ayyuha 'Lladhīna āmanū sallū ʿalayh." "Sallū"* is *faʿl amr,* an imperative verb (command): "O Believers! Praise the Prophet!" It is an order on every Muslim to praise the Prophet ﷺ continuously, non-stop. So when you stop, you are falling into forgetfulness of this *ayah* in which Allāh ﷻ ordered you to continuously recite *ṣalawāt* on the Prophet ﷺ. This is what distinguishes *awlīyāullāh* from normal people, as they are always praising the Prophet ﷺ because they are executing this *ayah, "Yā ayyuha 'Lladhīna* āmanū sallū 'alayhi wa sallimū taslīma," and they cannot stop because they have to do it.

That is like when Allāh ﷻ ordered the angels to make *sajda* to Sayyīdinā Adam ؑ:

وَإِذْ قُلْنَا لِلْمَلَائِكَةِ اسْجُدُوا لآدَمَ فَسَجَدُوا إِلاَّ إِبْلِيسَ

Wa idh qulnā li 'l-malā'ikatu 'sjudoo li ādama fa sajadoo illa Iblīs.

And when We told the angels, "Prostrate yourselves before Adam!" they all prostrated themselves, except Iblīs. (Sūrat al-Baqara, 2:34)

Allāh ﷻ said all of them made *sajda* except Iblīs. How many angels are there? In every moment Allāh is creating angels and He is "*al-Khāliq*," The Creator. You cannot say He created the angels and stopped. He ﷻ said, "Allāh and His angels are praising the Prophet." How many angels are praising the Prophet ﷺ? With respect to Allāh's Greatness and Grandeur, you cannot count and or know how many angels there are; they are an infinite number! Allāh ﷻ is creating angels every moment; not a million, a billion, a quadrillion, no! Allāh is creating infinite numbers of angels in every moment. His Name is "*al-Khāliq*," so if you say *khalq* stopped, you commit the sin of *kufr*, because Allāh ﷻ creates continuously!

Therefore, when He ordered the angels to make *sajda* to Sayyīdinā Adam ؑ, how many angels were there at that moment, then more were created and appeared, but how? They appeared already in *sajda*! They didn't come standing, because they are under that *khitāb*, address, when Allāh ﷻ ordered them to make the *sajda* of *ihtirām*, respect, not the *sajda* of *'ibādah*, worship, as worship is exclusively for Allāh ﷻ.

Sayyīdinā Yusuf ؑ came to his father, Sayyīdinā Yaqūb ؑ, and said:

إِنِّي رَأَيْتُ أَحَدَ عَشَرَ كَوْكَبًا وَالشَّمْسَ وَالْقَمَرَ رَأَيْتُهُمْ لِي سَاجِدِينَ

Innī rā'itu ihda 'ashar kawkaban wa 'sh-shamsa wa 'l-qamra rāytahum lī sājidīn.

I saw eleven planets and the sun and moon making sajda to me.

(Sūrat Yusuf, 12:5)

Such examples are to teach all of us. Sayyīdinā Yaqūb ؑ said, "Don't tell this to your brothers." They are all Prophets of Banī Isrā'īl, so how could they be jealous, because all Prophets are *ma'sūmūn*, infallible (without sin), although they threw Yusuf in the well. Another lesson for us is when Allāh ﷻ ordered His angels to make *sajda* to Sayyīdinā Adam ﷺ.

The Angels' Salawat is Continuous

Once I asked an *'alim* who is also a *mufti*, "Is there any verse in Holy Qur'an that ordered the angels to raise their head from their *sajda* to Sayyīdinā Adam ﷺ?" After you complete *sajda* you raise your head, but there is no mention of this in Holy Qur'an, because they are still in *sajda* to the Prophet ﷺ! That *'alim* said, "I didn't think of it like that because I am a scholar of Shari'ah, not *tasawwuf*." However, this is not from *tasawwuf*. In Holy Qur'an, Allāh ﷻ did not order His angels to raise their heads! Also, He ﷻ did not order them to make only one or two prostrations. If someone ordered you to make *sajda*, naturally you would wait to be told to raise your head, is it not?

That is why the Prophet ﷺ said in the *ḥadīth*, "Try to be excessive in *ṣalawāt* on me on the day and night of *Jumu'ah*," because *Jumu'ah* is the day Allāh ﷻ created Sayyīdinā Adam ﷺ, and the day he met with Sayyida Hawwa (Eve) ﷺ, and the day Adam was sent to Earth, and the day Allāh saved Sayyīdinā Nuh ﷺ from the flood, and the day Allāh saved Sayyīdinā 'Ibrāhīm ﷺ from the fire of Nimrod, and the day Allāh saved Banī Isrā'īl from Pharaoh, and it is the day when Allāh saved Sayyīdinā 'Isa ﷺ from his people that came to kill him.

Also, Allāh ﷻ gave *Jumu'ah* as a holy day to Sayyīdinā Muḥammad ﷺ! *Jumu'ah* is a precious day that contains all these benefits! On *Jumu'ah*, Allāh ﷻ sent you from Heaven to Earth and will send you from Earth to Heaven. It is the day to be saved by the Boat of Heaven and from Shayṭan, and the day to be saved from Fire. Sayyīdinā 'Isa ﷺ was raised to Paradise on *Jumu'ah*, the day the Prophet ﷺ liked most. The Day of Resurrection will be on a *Jumu'ah*. So every *Jumu'ah*, make as much praise on the Prophet ﷺ as you can, as he ﷺ said in a *ḥadīth*:

> *Anyone who praises me on the day and night of Jumu'ah, I will be a witness for him on the Day of Judgment and I will intercede for him.* (Jami' as-Saghīr)

We are ordered to send *ṣalawāt* on the Prophet ﷺ! From his mercy, he didn't order us to make a million *ṣalawāt*; he said to increase it, to recite more *ṣalawāt* than normal on *Jumu'ah.* So if you recite a hundred *ṣalawāt* daily, on *Jumu'ah r*ecite two-hundred *ṣalawāt;* if you normally recite two-hundred *ṣalawāt,* increase it to four-hundred on *Jumu'ah.* That is why in the *awrād* assigned by Mawlana Shaykh Nazim ق, on *Jumu'ah* beginners increase their daily recitation of *ṣalawāt* from one-hundred to five-hundred.

It is mentioned that whoever recites *ṣalawāt* on the Prophet ﷺ a hundred times will be forgiven the sins of 80 years! Now it is coming out; the easement is granted and they are giving you a way out of the daily responsibility to recite *ṣalawāt* two-hundred, five-hundred or a thousand times! Now, if today is *Jumu'ah* and you recite one-hundred *ṣalawāt* on Prophet ﷺ, eighty years of sins will be erased, then next week again recite one-hundred *ṣalawāt* and another eighty years of sins will be erased! This is how in previous times people encouraged their followers to do *ṣalawāt* on the Prophet ﷺ, but today, although many people do it, but the *ummah* is sleeping and most of us are not remembering this important *sunnah.*

This is an account of a woman who came to a big *wali,* Hasan al-Basri ؓ, whose lineage is connected to Sayyīdinā 'Alī ؓ through Sayyīdinā Ja'far as-Sādiq ؓ. The title "Naqshbandi Golden Chain" is from the combined lineage of Sayyīdinā 'Alī ق and Sayyīdinā Abu Bakr as-Siddiq ق that came together in their descendant, Sayyīdinā Ja'far as-Sādiq ق. So this *ṭarīqat* is coming from two sides. The Shi'a call themselves "Ja'fari" as they take from Sayyīdinā Ja'far. Sayyīdinā Qassim ؓ, the grandson of Abu Bakr as-Siddiq ؓ, gave to Sayyīdinā Ja'far, who also took from Hasan al-Basri ؓ, who is taking from Sayyīdinā 'Alī ق, whereas the Prophet ﷺ said:

أنا مدينة العلم و علي بابه

Anā madinatu 'l-'ilmi wa 'alīyyun bābuha.

I am the City of Knowledge and 'Alī is it's door. (al-Hākim, Tirmidhi)

It is also related, what some say is *ḥadīth* and some say it is not a *ḥadīth,* that the Prophet ﷺ said:

Ma sabb-Allāhu fī sadrī sababatahu fī sadra abi bakr as-siddiq.

Whatever Allāh has poured in my heart, I poured in the heart of Abu Bakr as-Siddiq.

So in Sayyīdinā Jaʿfar as-Sādiq ﷺ we are getting the two connections, from Sayyīdinā Abu Bakr as-Siddiq ﷺ and from Sayyīdinā ʿAlī ﷺ, and that is why it is called the "Golden Chain".

I now quote from the book *Manahij as-Saʿadāt*, page 5, by al-Hafizh as-Sakhāwi, a very famous scholar in classical, traditional Islam:

> A woman came to Hasan al-Basri and said, "One of my daughters died and I very much want to see her in a dream."[7] He told her, "Pray *Ṣalāt al-ʿIsha*; then pray four *rakaʿats* and in every *rakaʿat* read *Sūrat al-Fātiḥah* and *Sūrat at-Takāthur*. Then go to sleep directly and sleep completely; you will see her in your dream." She returned and said, "I did that and saw her in my dream. She was in punishment and torture!" (It might be the daughter did something wrong in her life.) She was dressed in a dress of *qitrān*, burning hot tar, and her arms and legs were bound with chains of fire!"

What kind of extreme punishment is that? Look how we are backbiting and cursing each other! Everyone must be busy auditing himself; make an account of yourself, don't punch this one and that one. Also, don't take words of others out of context; for example, when I recently said, "In 2003, when Mawlana Shaykh retired from traveling..." some accused me of having said, "In 2003, when Mawlana Shaykh 'retired'..." without completing the statement (and by that they made *fitna* among *murīds*). Don't they remember that Allāh ﷻ said:

يَا أَيُّهَا الَّذِينَ آمَنُوا إِن جَاءكُمْ فَاسِقٌ بِنَبَأٍ فَتَبَيَّنُوا أَن تُصِيبُوا قَوْمًا بِجَهَالَةٍ فَتُصْبِحُوا عَلَى مَا فَعَلْتُمْ نَادِمِينَ

Yā ayyuha 'Lladhīna āmanū in ja'akum fāsiqun bi naba'in fa-tabayyinū an tusībū qawman bi-jahālatin fatusbihū ʿalā mā faʿltum nādimīn.

O you who believe! If a corrupt person comes to you with something wrong, ascertain the truth unless you harm people unwittingly and afterwards become full of repentance for what you have done. (Sūrat al-Ḥujurāt, 49:6)

[7] There are books of sacred recitations and numerous *awliyaullāh* wrote what one must recite to see the Prophet (s) in the dream, which we will discuss in this series.

I praised Mawlana Shaykh Nazim ق and made a point about when he retired from traveling, as the Prophet ﷺ told Grandshaykh ʿAbdAllāh ق after his *khalwat* in *Madinat al-Munawwara,* "You don't need to go after people now; I will send the *mukhlis,* the best people will come to you." After that people from all over the world came to Grandshaykh ق and then to Mawlana Shaykh Nazim ق. The evidence is that you cannot find two people here from the same country; turn to camera to show who are here.

The Prophet ﷺ said:

تعرض علي أعمالكم فان رأيت خيرا حمدت الله تعالى وإن رأيت شرا استغفرت لكم

Tuʿradu ʿalayya ʿamalakum fa in rā'itu khayran hamadta 'Llāh wa in rā'itu sharran astaghfarta lahum.

I observe the deeds of my ummah. If I find good I thank Allāh, and if I see other than that, bad, I ask forgiveness for them.

So how can a *wali* "retire"? How can they mention such a thing on *Jumuʿah*? Was it said or not? They took one word, as if someone said, *"lā ilāha,"* but did not say, *"illa-Llāh,"* which is *kufr*; you cannot say *"lā ilāha"* without saying *"illa-Llāh."* Say now, *"Lā ilāha illa-Llāh Muḥammadan Rasūlullāh!"*

Today and until the last day of his life at 150 years *inshā-Allāh,* may Mawlana Shaykh Nazim al-Haqqani ق give *ṣuḥbah*! So how is he 'retired' as they said? The one who repeated that lie was supposed to check it first; that is his mistake. But the one who whispered it in his ear out of context committed the sin of *namīma,* to spread a false rumor, to say what is not true but make it seem correct, which is worse than *ghībat,* to backbite!

Hasan al-Basri ق replied to the distressed mother, "Give *sadaqa* on her behalf and *inshā-Allāh,* Allāh ﷻ will forgive her." The way he said it indicated, "Give *sadaqa* for her and I will distribute it." This is an important point. When a shaykh distributes *sadaqa,* it is not like when a normal person does so, as it is written in Holy Qur'an, that if you do something wrong go to the Prophet ﷺ:

وَلَوْ أَنَّهُمْ إِذ ظَّلَمُوا أَنفُسَهُمْ جَاءُوكَ فَاسْتَغْفَرُوا اللَّهَ وَاسْتَغْفَرَ لَهُمُ الرَّسُولُ لَوَجَدُوا اللَّهَ تَوَّابًا رَّحِيمًا

Wa law annahum idh zhalamū anfusahum ja'ūka f 'astaghfarūllāha w 'astaghfarallāhumu 'r-rasūlu la-wajadū 'Llāha tawwāba 'r-raḥīma.

If they had only, when they were unjust to themselves, come to you and asked Allāh's forgiveness, and the Messenger had asked forgiveness for them, they would have found Allāh indeed Oft-returning, Most Merciful.

(Sūrat an-Nisa, 4:64)

If you make a mistake, you have to go to the Prophet ﷺ or to his inheritors to remedy that situation. Like that lady asked, "What should I do?" and Hasan al-Basri said, "Give *sadaqa*." We know the *Ṣaḥābah* came to the Prophet ﷺ and asked forgiveness in his presence, but Allāh ﷻ put another condition, that on your behalf the Prophet ﷺ will also ask Allāh ﷻ for His Forgiveness!

> That lady made *sadaqa*, and then Hasan al-Basri said, "May Allāh forgive her." That night, Hasan al-Basri slept and he found himself in one of the Paradises where he saw a bed on which a very beautiful lady sat, and on her head was a crown of light. [This is an account from Hasan al-Basri ؓ, not from you or me throwing some words around with no origin, or (invented) words from the sky!] He looked at her and was stunned.
>
> She said (casually), "*Yā* Hasan! Do you know me?" He did not use his spiritual power from the Prophet ﷺ to get that information. She said, "I am the daughter of that woman whom you ordered to pray on the Prophet ﷺ in order to see me in the dream!"
>
> Sayyīdinā Hasan ؓ said, "But your mother came to me and told me she saw you in a different way than this, so what happened? You were in punishment and just ten hours later, in my dream I am seeing you in Paradise!"[8]
>
> She said, "Yes, my mother spoke the truth."
>
> He asked, "How did you reach this level?"
>
> She said, "We were 70,000 people in this kind of punishment and I was one among them, it is true. Then a pious man like you, one *wali, rajulun min as-sālihīn*, passed by our graves in the cemetery and recited praise

---

[8] Sayyidina Hasan al-Basri ق came 100 years after the Prophet (s) and through this account wanted to teach his followers.

on the Prophet ﷺ one time, and we all heard him. And he asked Allāh ﷻ and the Prophet ﷺ, 'Grant the reward of this to the bodies in these graves.' Then Allāh ﷻ accepted his *du'a* and released all of us from that punishment!"

That is an account of the power of one recitation of *ṣalawāt 'ala an-Nabī* ﷺ! Say now, *"Allāhumma salli 'alā Sayyīdinā Muḥammad wa 'alā āli Sayyīdinā Muḥammad*!" With that, we are now free from Hellfire! That is why *ṣalawāt* is important and why scholars of Islam teach that when you pass by a cemetery, recite one-hundred times *"Qul Huwa Allāhu Ahad* (*Sūrat al-Ikhlās*)," and one-hundred times *ṣalawāt 'ala an-Nabī* ﷺ.

May Allāh ﷻ forgive us and may Allāh ﷻ bless us.

Wa min Allāhi 't-tawfiq, bi ḥurmati 'l-ḥabīb, bi ḥurmati 'l-Fātiḥah.

And with Allāh is success. For the sake of the Beloved, for his sake we recite the opening chapter of Holy Qur'an.

Genuine Inspiration is from Prophet and is Always Clear

Aʿūdhu billāhi min ash-Shayṭāni 'r-rajīm. Bismillāhi' r-Raḥmāni 'r-Raḥīm.
Nawaytu 'l-arbāʿīn, nawaytu 'l-ʿitikāf, nawaytu'l-khalwah, nawaytu 'l-ʿuzlah,
nawaytu 'r-riyāḍa, nawaytu 's-sulūk, lillāhi Taʿalā fī hādhā 'l-masjid.
Atīʿūllāha wa atīʿū 'r-Rasūla wa ūlī 'l-amri minkum.
Obey Allāh, obey the Prophet, and obey those in authority among you. (4:59)

Dastūr, madad yā Sulṭān al-Awlīyā, Mawlana Shaykh Nazim al-Haqqani ق.
Dastūr, madad yā Sulṭān al-Awlīyā, Mawlana Shaykh ʿAbdAllāh ad-Daghestani ق.

We are asking for their *madad* to reach the Prophet ﷺ. Although many people claim to have reached the Prophet ﷺ and to get inspirations from him, it is not that easy. Nowadays the word "inspiration" has become so easy on the tongue; everyone is saying, "I have an inspiration." However, did they ever stop to think whether their inspirations are true or false? How can you recognize if an inspiration is real and true? It is not so easy for anyone to say unless they have been granted this by Allāh ﷻ, such as *awlīyāullāh*, as mentioned in the Holy Qur'an:

فَأَلْهَمَهَا فُجُورَهَا وَتَقْوَاهَا

Fa alhamahā fujūrahā wa taqwāhā.
He inspired the self of its good and its bad. *(Sūrat ash-Shams, 91:8)*

You cannot say you have an "inspiration" when in reality you didn't, so don't lie! That is why *awlīyāullāh* know how difficult it is to say, "I have an inspiration." It has been mentioned in numerous places in the Holy Qur'an that Allāh ﷻ sends dreams, like the one He sent to Sayyīdinā 'Ibrāhīm ﷺ, ordering him to sacrifice his son. Despite this, Sayyīdinā 'Ibrāhīm ﷺ did not say, "It was an inspiration," which is something that comes directly from Allāh ﷻ through the Prophet ﷺ! In fact, Mawlana Shaykh Nazim ق usually says, "I went to rest and had a dream." He never says, "I am getting an inspiration," as he is so humble.

Although *awlīyāullāh* receive inspirations from the Prophet ﷺ at every moment, due to their *adab* and respect of the Prophet ﷺ, they never claim it until they show the highest level of helplessness in front of him ﷺ, saying, "*Yā Sayyidī*! Not until we lie down and receive an inspiration from you will we speak on it!" This is proper *adab*, which you must display in every move you make. It is said, *aṭ-ṭarīqatu kullāhā adab*, "All of *ṭarīqah* is discipline." An example of good *adab* is that one must not use the *tasbīḥ* when the shaykh is speaking. You may use hundreds of beads during your own time, but when Mawlana Shaykh Nazim is speaking you must not use it as the Prophet ﷺ prohibited us to touch beads or anything when the *Imam* is on the pulpit giving *khutbah*:

من مسح الحجر فقد لغي

Man massa 'l-hajar faqad laghā.

Whoever touches a pebble (during khutbah) has committed a foolish act.

(Abu Dawud, *Fadl al-Jumuʿah)*

So any movement during that is considered *laghaw*, absolutely disliked, and they are making a mistake in their religion. When the *Imam* is on the *minbar*, there are many who use their beads or put their hands in their pockets to turn off their cell phones even while they are praying, which is *laghaw*. It is much better to turn off your cell phone before the *ṣuḥbah* or *khutbah* starts; also, if it rings during prayer don't move, let it ring, because three movements during prayer invalidate it.

عن أنس رضي الله عنه قال: قال رسول الله صلى الله عليه وسلم: انصر أخاك ظالماً أو مظلوماً، فقال: رجل يا رسول الله صلى الله عليه وسلم أنصره إذ كان مظلوماً، أفرأيت إذا كان ظالماً كيف أنصره؟! قال: تحجزه أو تمنعه من الظلم، فإن ذلك نصره

Qāla Rasūlullāh ﷺ ansur akhāka zhāliman aw mazhlūman, faqāl rajulun: Yā rasūlullāh ﷺ ansurhu idh kāna mazhlūman, afarā'ita idhā kāna zhāliman kayfa ansuruh? Qāla: tahjizahu aw tamnaʿahu min azh-zhulm, fa inna dhalika nasruh.

The Prophet ﷺ said, "Help your brother, whether he is an oppressor or is oppressed," after which a man asked, "O Messenger of Allāh! I know how to help my brother when he is oppressed, but how can I help him when he is an oppressor?" He said, "You can restrain him from committing oppression. That will be your help to him." (Bukhari)

The Ṣaḥābah ؓ asked, "How can we support our brother when he is oppressing?" We understand that people come to the shaykh when they are oppressed in their lives; you might be oppressed by your wife, your father, your sister or your brother, and so the shaykh will try to make you feel good. The Ṣaḥābah ؓ said, "Yā Rasūlullāh ﷺ! We understand about the oppressed, but what to do for the oppressor?" So the Prophet ﷺ said, "Support him by telling him his mistakes, and that, 'What you are saying is incorrect.'"

For example, if someone whispered in your ear by phone before or after the lecture, they are using you like a horse to deliver something. They use you! You made a mistake, so try to avoid repeating it and next time, try to prevent your brother from falling into the same mistake! That is how you support him, by preventing him from becoming an oppressor, when you tell him, "Be careful, as what is being said is not true and they are using you to spread *fitna*, *ghībah* or *namīma,* which the Prophet ﷺ prohibited."

The Prophet ﷺ asked, "Who is the bankrupted?" The Ṣaḥābah said, "The one with no wealth," and the Prophet ﷺ said, "No, Allāh ﷻ still provides sustenance for the one with no wealth," even to the homeless. Once in San Francisco … I saw one homeless person … (who) was happy with his simple life while we are not, although Allāh ﷻ gave us everything! Still we are backbiting each other! This one says, "I will take your picture," and the other says, "You are there so I will not bring my camera," as if the camera is going to make you an important personality. The camera is an instrument used to propagate Mawlana Shaykh's name, so if we have a hundred cameras here, it is better than having ten cameras, because every camera has its own audience and each one channels to different people with different goals.

It is not right that they make it look like enemies are here in Mawlana's house! We are coming here to be together in our happiness, not to impose rules, such as "this one has permission to see the shaykh and, but that one does not have permission." No, it is by intention: from the moment you leave your house saying, "I am going for *Sunnah*," the *Sunnah* is written for you whether you reach it or not! If you make the intention to go for *ziyarah* to the Prophet ﷺ and prepare all the necessary documents, and you take one step out of the house and get involved in an accident, the reward will still be written for you!

Similarly, it is written for anyone who steps out to visit a *masjid*, or to go for *ziyarah* to the grave of a *wali*. So what do you think if you are stepping out to visit a living shaykh? You will be rewarded as soon as you step out of your house and it is written that you visited him and returned and Allāh ﷻ will reward you! What about if you are visiting *Sulṭān al-Awlīyā,* Mawlana Shaykh Muḥammad Nazim Adil al-Haqqani? Is there any enmity anymore? This is an ocean and we are diving in it! When you go to the ocean, what do you see? What is the color of the ocean? Do you see anything else? To see more, you need to dive into the ocean, then you will see how everything completely changes into a colorful scenery and you will begin to witness nature's beauty as you have never witnessed on Earth.

Allāh's Creation of the ocean is miraculous and as you dive further, you see more and more. So when you go to a *masjid*, will Allāh ﷻ not grant you to see more than what He gave ocean divers? It is not just limited to seeing the *minbar*, the cabinets and the people here and there. In reality, Allāh ﷻ will make you dive in the ocean of that Sultan you visited: you are diving in his heart! He will take you in his heart to wherever he is in the presence of the Prophet ﷺ! Allāh ﷻ granted *awlīyāullāh* unlimited power, so do not underestimate the Greatness that He gave to His Prophet ﷺ, to the *Ṣaḥābah* ؓ, to *al-a'immah* and to *awlīyāullāh*. But sadly, we are blind.

You cannot dive into the ocean without the help of certain instruments, such as goggles and an oxygen tank, or you might drown. Goggles will help you see and oxygen is the gas of life. Everything in this universe is in the form of gas that originates from energy. When Allāh ﷻ said "*Kun*!" everything came in the form of gas and took its shape. Hydrogen and oxygen make you live, and both elements come together to form water. Here "oxygen" refers to the knowledge, the sophisticated rocket that *awlīyāullāh* put on your shoulders through the *awrād* and their love to you and your love to them. That is why people say to each other "You are my oxygen," meaning "I cannot live without you." *Awlīyāullāh* are the oxygen of this life and without them there is only darkness.

وَمَن كَانَ فِي هَٰذِهِ أَعْمَىٰ فَهُوَ فِي الْآخِرَةِ أَعْمَىٰ وَأَضَلُّ سَبِيلًا

Wa man kāna fi hadhihi ʿamā fa-huwa fi 'l-ākhirati ʿamā wa adallū sabīla.

But those who were blind in this world will be blind in the Hereafter and most stray from the path. (Sūrat al-Isrā', 17:72)

That is why *awlīyāullāh* give you the *awrād* first as they don't want you to be blind, and they say, "These are your goggles," then they give you the oxygen, saying, "Use these *awrād* and we can show you what you cannot see with your eyes!"

Prophet ﷺ said:

ولا يزال عبدي يتقرب إلي بالنوافل حتى أحبه، فإذا أحببته كنت سمعه الذي يسمع به وبصره الذي يبصر به، ويده التي يبطش بها ورجله التي يمشي بها،

Wa lā yazāla ʿabdī yataqarabu ilayya bi' n-nawāfil hatta uhibbah. Fa idhā ahbābtahu kuntu samaʿuhulladhī yasmaʿu bihi wa basarahulladhī yubsiru bihi, wa yadahulladhī yabtishu bihā wa rijlahullatī yamshī bihā.

My servant does not cease to approach Me through voluntary worship until I will love him. When I love him, I will become the ears with which he hears, the eyes with which he sees, the hand with which he acts, and the legs with which he walks (and other versions include, "and the tongue with which he speaks.").

(*Ḥadīth Qudsī*, Bukhari)

Allāh ﷻ is saying, *fa idhā ahbābtahu*, "If I love him;" (there is an "if" there), which means you have to keeping running and asking until Allāh ﷻ loves you. And when Allāh ﷻ is saying, "He approaches me through voluntary worship until I love him," that means Allāh loves you, because all of you here are coming from long distances to see the shaykh, which is voluntary worship. Why else are you coming here, but for Allāh! He ﷻ loves us and, therefore, He brought us together. Those present here are lucky and those absent are lucky as well, because their spirits are present. Any follower of Mawlana Shaykh Nazim ق around the world is present here; we cannot say "no," as that would be diminishing the power of the shaykh, who can reach anyone. He doesn't need you to reach him, he reaches you! Allāh ﷻ said, "If I love him, then I will be the ears that he can hear with."

Islam is Based on Obedience

That means you will hear what people cannot hear. Just now we were speaking about instruments such as various computer chips that can hear (spy); according to an article I recently read, now there are computer chips in everything, not only in phones, and they can release your voice and hear what is happening even if the phone is off!

That is why you have to be loyal to your country and abide by its laws. Grandshaykh ق used to always recite that *ayah*:

أَطِيعُوا اللهَ وَأَطِيعُوا الرَّسُولَ وَأُولِي الأَمْرِ مِنكُمْ

Atīʿūllāha wa atīʿū 'r-Rasūla wa ūlī 'l-amri minkum.

Obey Allāh, obey the Prophet, and obey those in authority among you.

(Sūrat an-Nisa, 4:59)

I remember something that perhaps only Shaykh Adnan knows, that Grandshaykh ق used to say, "I always pray for Hafiz al-Assad (former President of Syria)." Why? Because you have to obey the law. If Allāh ﷻ put him over us, we have to obey. If I live in the west, I have to obey and love the west; if I live in Europe, I have to love Europe; if I live in the east, I have to love the east, because the Prophet ﷺ said:

حب الوطن من الايمان

Hubb al-watan min al-imān.

Love of the homeland is part of faith.

So don't come against your government or you will lose; just surrender, as we are normal and peaceful students of Mawlana Shaykh Nazim ق. I remember during the Lebanese War, Mawlana Shaykh never allowed us to carry a weapon, although everyone had weapons there and not just guns, but also rockets, tanks, and RPGs. He did not let us carry even a knife, although it is a *sunnah*, but he did not want it to be written in the *Lawh al-Mahfouzh* that we carried a weapon!

Islam is obedience, so when you obey Allāh ﷻ, His Messenger, and those in authority as mentioned in the above *ayāh*, Allāh ﷻ will give you "eyes to see what no one can see, ears to hear what no one can hear, a tongue to say things no one can say," and He will give you hands that can move mountains! Let us go into this a bit further. If you have one ton of iron or metal and someone tells you to carry it from here to there, you cannot. You would need a machine, a crane to help you perform that task. But still, if you don't give it electricity or gasoline in it, what will the crane do? Nothing, as it will not be able to carry that load. But if you connect it to electricity or put gasoline, the crane will be able to lift one, two, or three tons.

Electricity and gasoline sources of energy. Grandshaykh ق said Allāh ﷻ gave energy to *awlīyāullāh* that if they say to the mountain, "Move," it will move! Which is better, energy of this universe or energy that Allāh ﷻ gave to people? Everything in this universe is made of energy. If you look at the Periodic Table, every atom consists of mass and energy: the electrons, protons, neutron and the mass. We are consisting of both *rūh* or energy, and body, the mass.

If you reach that energy you can do something different, just as Sayyīdinā ʿUmar ؓ once spoke on the *minbar* in Madinah, addressing his commander Sārīyya in Damascus, who was 3,000 km away. Sayyīdinā ʿUmar saw and heard, whereas Sayyīdinā Sārīyya ؓ only heard his voice, telling him, "Go to the mountain! They are coming from behind the mountain!" Sayyīdinā Umar ؓ was at a higher level, hearing and seeing the enemy coming from behind the mountain. Although Sayyīdinā ʿUmar ؓ is not a prophet, he was able to see. When Allāh wants, He will give to whomever He likes! Thus, He gave to *awlīyāullāh*, to Mawlana Shaykh Nazim ق, and we have to learn from what they say.

Let us now see what the shaykh al-Islam of the Shafiʿī school of thought, who was also the Grand Mufti of Mecca, wrote in his book *Taqrīb wusūl ila ʿilm al-usūl*. As previously discussed, we have to accept what *awlīyā* say because they cannot lie on the Prophet ﷺ; when they see the Prophet ﷺ in a dream and he tells them, "Do this or that," the matter is finished and they cannot lie. He said: "I saw the Prophet ﷺ," [he didn't say 'in a dream' or 'in a vision,' which means it can be both, because in other places they say *ra'aitu an-Nabī ﷺ fir-ruyā*, "I saw the Prophet ﷺ in a dream."] So he said, "I saw the Prophet ﷺ and asked him, '*Yā Rasūlullāh*! You said that Allāh prays ten times on the one who makes prayer on you once, correct?'" as we know the Prophet ﷺ said in an authentic *ḥadīth*:

من صلى علي واحدة صلى الله عليه عشرا

Man salla ʿalayya marratan sal-Allāhu bihā ʿalayha ʿashr.

If anyone invokes a blessing on me once, Allāh will grant him ten blessings.

(Bukhari and Muslim)

So he continued, *hal hadha in kāna hādir al-qalb,* "But does that require the presence of the heart (such as while meditating)?" Many people ask about meditation in Islam, unaware that Allāh ﷻ said in the Holy Qur'an:

الَّذِينَ يَذْكُرُونَ اللّهَ قِيَامًا وَقُعُودًا وَعَلَىَ جُنُوبِهِمْ وَيَتَفَكَّرُونَ فِي خَلْقِ السَّمَاوَاتِ وَالأَرْضِ رَبَّنَا مَا خَلَقْتَ هَذا بَاطِلاً سُبْحَانَكَ فَقِنَا عَذَابَ النَّارِ

Alladhīna yadhkurūnullāha qiyamān wa quʿūdan wa ʿalā junūbihim wa yattafakkarūna fī khalqi 's-samāwāti wa 'l-ardi rabbanā mā khalaqta hadhā bātilan subḥānaka fa qinā ʿadhāba 'n-nār.

Those who remember Allāh (always, and in prayers) standing, sitting, and lying down on their sides, and think deeply about the Creation of the Heavens and the Earth, (saying) "Our Lord! You have not created (all) this without purpose! Glory to You! Give us salvation from the torment of the Fire."

(Sūrat Āli ʿImrān, 3:191)

Allāh ﷻ is saying, "Those who make *dhikr* standing, sitting and lying down, *wa yatafakkarūn*, and they contemplate on the Creation of the Heavens and Earth." Allāh said, "contemplate" or "meditate" on the Holy Qur'an! Not only that, but the Prophet ﷺ also said:

تفكر ساعة خير من عبادة سبعين سنة

Tafakkarru saʿatin khayrun min ʿibādati sabaʿīn sannah.

To remember Allāh ﷻ for one hour (contemplate or meditate) is better than seventy years of worship.

If you sit on your knees thinking about the Creation of Heavens and Earth, or about the Holy Qur'an and holy *ḥadīth,* and make *dhikrullāh,* you will be rewarded the worship of seventy years, which is a third of your life completed in worship! Did I say something wrong? If I did, correct me, we are all at the same door.

One time I was going to Malaysia with Mawlana Shaykh Nazim ق and he said to me, "Look at my turban; it is (symbolically) covered with all different kinds of jewels, diamonds, sapphires, emeralds and rubies. If one of these jewels is out of place, my turban will look bad!" So we are all the same; I cannot claim to be higher because I am giving a lecture, no! If Mawlana wants to pull it, he may do so in one second. How many *awlīyāullāh* pulled that from their *murīds* to teach them *adab*? So don't claim anything is from yourself, as they can pull it at any moment and then give it back to show you your weakness.

Also, don't say, "It is inspiration." I didn't explain this point before, but it is very important. Sometimes when you see a fuzzy picture on the television, it is difficult to understand what you are actually seeing, which may be traces of something, but nothing much. However, if your connection is good, you will get a very clear picture and sound. So don't say, "I have an inspiration (as if that legitimizes what you are saying)," because you cannot cheat me on that, for while it may be an inspiration it is still fuzzy, so don't speak about it as you might be wrong.

Here I will mention the example Grandshaykh ق gave us about the four *madhhāhib*, schools of Islamic jurisprudence, because in Islam every claim must be traced back to a source. A brief history of the Four Schools of Thought is: Imam Abu Hanifa ؓ first brought the Hanafi *madhhab*, second was Imam Malik ؓ with the Maliki *madhhab*, third was Imam Shafi'i ؓ with the Shafi'i *madhhab*, and fourth was Imam Ahmad bin Hanbal ؓ with the Hanbali *madhhab*, with two-hundred years between them. Their followers used to fight with each other because each group supported their own school of thought.

So one time Grandshaykh ق said, "How do I describe the four *madhāhib*, schools of thought? If they ask me if these four *Imams* explained Shari'ah completely, I will say, 'Yes, they explained Shari'ah in detail.' But according to Imam Shafi'i, when he was in Baghdad, he recorded his *madhhab* in the book, *Kitāb al-Umm, The Mother (Exemplar) of Books*, which is perhaps thirty volumes, but when went to Egypt in the later years of his life, he had to modify his school of thought from the original because he saw more corruption in Egypt." So that tells us there is a fuzzy picture. When Imam Shafi'i was in Baghdad he saw everything good, but upon his arrival in Egypt, he found more corruption and so he made his *madhhab* more strict. Similarly, if you go from Imam Abu Hanifa to Imam Malik to Imam Shafi'i and end with Imam Ahmad, as corruption increased the teachings gradually became more and more strict.

So what then do you think would be the *madhhab* of today? Still we say, "It is inspiration," and *alhamdulillāh*, we accept that, but don't say it regarding something you know is wrong, especially if it is an inspiration that might jeopardize the system, the entire *ṭarīqah*. You cannot do that! I have heard Mawlana Shaykh Nazim ق say many times that this one (his grandson) is very sincere, very pious, has good *imān* and is a very strong supporter, so if he tells me, "I have an inspiration," I say okay (accept that), but if he tells me he has an inspiration that this book I am quoting from is wrong, I cannot accept it (as it is an authentic source of Islamic knowledge)!

On the first Monday of every month, all the scholars of Damascus would visit Grandshaykh ʿAbdAllāh ق and then perform *ziyarah* at the *maqām* of Sayyīdinā Khalid al-Baghdadi ق. Grandshaykh ق said to them, "If they ask me to describe the Four Schools of Thought, I will describe it this way. I would ask, 'Can you see that mountain (Jabal Qasiyoun)? There is an animal standing on top of that mountain. Can you see it?' If they ask me what kind of animal it is, I will say, 'It is an animal.' But is it a goat, a sheep, a cow, or an ox?"

Just as we believe this is a book, but what is the book about? In order to review the book, I have to go through its pages. So he was telling those scholars, "I have to go up to the top of the mountain and then hold the animal's legs and arms, then I can confirm that it is an animal with four legs, because I saw and touched them. Then I will look into his face and see the eyes, mouth and nose, and I will know what kind of animal it is, whether it is deformed, the color of its skin, the ears and so forth. I have to describe it very well in order to say what I'm seeing is correct."

Who is doing that today? *Ṭarīqah* is to examine something very well by checking it, point by point in detail, not just to believe something through hearsay, as we cited previously:

يَا أَيُّهَا الَّذِينَ آمَنُوا إِن جَاءكُمْ فَاسِقٌ بِنَبَأٍ فَتَبَيَّنُوا أَن تُصِيبُوا قَوْمًا بِجَهَالَةٍ فَتُصْبِحُوا عَلَى مَا فَعَلْتُمْ نَادِمِينَ

Yā ayyuha 'Lladhīna āmanū in ja'akum fāsiqun bi naba'in fa-tabayyinū an tusībū qawman bi-jahālatin fatusbihū ʿalā mā faʿltum nādimīn.

O you who believe! If a corrupt person comes to you with something wrong, ascertain the truth unless you harm people unwittingly and afterwards become full of repentance for what you have done. (Sūrat al-Ḥujurāt, 49:6)

Allāh ﷻ didn't say, "O Human Beings!" He is addressing the believers: *Yā ayyuha 'Lladhīna āmanū*, "O Believers!" which indicates that we must always verify. "If a corrupt person comes to you with a news, don't believe it, check it." Usually people don't check it, and out of ignorance they might attack others, which is *ghībat* or *namīmah*. "Then you might end up in regret." If you do that, you are not going to be perfect, especially if you are an *ʿalim* or shaykh. Therefore, you must always verify the information, like politicians and media outlets and newspapers, as most of them do not tell the truth. You cannot lie, either in religion in general or in *tasawwuf*. So what did scholars of that time say?

According to the book, *Talkhīs al-Maʿarif, Summarizing the Knowledges* by Muḥammad ʿArif:

> Shaykh Zayni ad-Dahlan, who passed away 200 years ago, asked (in his dream), "*Yā Rasūlullāh!* You said Allāh ﷻ sends ten *ṣalawāt* on the one who makes one *ṣalawāt* on you. Does the heart need to be present?" Sometimes you might make *ṣalawāt* while listening to a talk or watching TV, saying, "*Allāhumma salli ʿalā Sayyīdinā Muḥammadin wa ʿalā āli Sayyīdinā Muḥammad.*" Is the heart present then? No, it is not. So he asked, "Does your heart have to be present or not?" The Prophet ﷺ said, "No, it is not necessary. Even if the person making *ṣalawāt* on me is *ghāfil*, heedless, and his heart is not connected, it will suffice; you can do *ṣalawāt* on me even though your heart is not present. Not only that, but Allāh ﷻ will give him mountains of angels who will make *istighfār* on his behalf and pray for him. And for the person whose heart is present, no one will know or can imagine what Allāh ﷻ will give him; that is only in Allāh's Knowledge!"

Look at the mercy of Allāh ﷻ, and also, do you see how much mercy the Prophet ﷺ is giving? Look how much you must love Sayyīdinā Muḥammad ﷺ! And our shaykh, his ﷺ representative, gave his life for the Prophet ﷺ, walking from one village in Syria to another to give *daʿwah*! Go and read it in the *Naqshbandi Sufi Way*. That reward for saying *ṣalawāt* one time, "*Allāhumma salli ʿalā Sayyīdinā Muḥammad wa ʿalā āli Sayyīdinā Muḥammad wa sallim*!" Look at the Greatness of Sayyīdinā Muḥammad ﷺ!

May Allāh ﷻ forgive us and may Allāh ﷻ bless us.

Wa min Allāhi 't-tawfīq, bi ḥurmati 'l-ḥabīb, bi ḥurmati 'l-Fātiḥah.

And with Allāh is success. For the sake of the Beloved, for his sake we recite the opening chapter of Holy Qur'an.

How Shaykh Sharafuddin's Life was Extended

Aʿūdhu billāhi min ash-Shayṭāni 'r-rajīm. Bismillāhi' r-Raḥmāni 'r-Raḥīm.
Nawaytu 'l-arbāʿīn, nawaytu 'l-ʿitikāf, nawaytu'l-khalwah, nawaytu 'l-ʿuzlah,
nawaytu 'r-riyāḍa, nawaytu 's-sulūk, lillāhi Taʿālā fī hādhā 'l-masjid.
Atīʿūllāha wa atīʿū 'r-Rasūla wa ūlī 'l-amri minkum.
Obey Allāh, obey the Prophet, and obey those in authority among you. (4:59)

Dastūr, madad yā Sulṭān al-Awlīyā, Mawlana Shaykh Nazim al-Haqqani ق.
Dastūr, madad yā Sulṭān al-Awlīyā, Mawlana Shaykh ʿAbdAllāh ad-Daghestani ق.

We previously related a *ḥadīth* narrated by Imam Tirmidhi ؓ where the Prophet ﷺ mentions that Allāh ﷻ stroked the back of Sayyīdinā Adam ﵇, and all his *dhurriyya,* atoms (of his descendants) came out. They had lights shining from their foreheads. Then Sayyīdinā Adam ﵇ liked one of this *dhurriyya* who had special light coming from his forehead and he asked, "*Yā Rabb*! Who is that one?" and Allāh ﷻ answered, "That is one of your descendants that will come in a later *ummah.*" Sayyīdinā Adam ﵇ said he liked that one and he pledged, "O my Lord! Give forty years of my life to him." When the Angel of Death ﵇ came to take Sayyīdinā Adam's life, Adam said, "You came early," then Allāh ﷻ reminded him, "No, you forgot that you gave him (your *dhurriyya*) from your life."

That *ḥadīth* is *ḥasan saḥih,* which means it is highly sound and unquestionable, not *daʿīf,* questionable. There are thirty-five different categories of *ḥadīth,* and only scholars can understand these things. I mentioned this in 1991, when I debated Shaykh Muḥammad Adly, a member of *Rābitah al-ʿAlam al-Islāmi* (Muslim World League), in an open debate on the Internet about the existence of *tasawwuf* in Islam. We had that debate before anyone even knew about the Internet. He was in New York and I was in California.

So from this and other examples, we see there are cases where a *murīd* gave from his life to his shaykh. Also, there are cases where a shaykh gave his life to his *murīd.* Is it correct? Why are you keeping quiet? In Egypt, in a *majlis* of learning such as this one, if a scholar asks you something and you say nothing, the scholar will close the *majlis*! Don't be like a statue. What do you say, is it correct? Yes? (Yes sir!) When you say, "Yes sir!" it means it is confirmed.

So I asked Mawlana Shaykh Nazim, may Allāh give him long life, to give us more proofs and he reminded me about the story of Shaykh Zia and Shaykh Sharafuddin ق. Have you heard it? It is Mawlana's story, included in the Naqshbandi Sufi Way.

Once Shaykh Sharafuddin ق went to Istanbul and stayed at the Hotel Massarat, which means "Happy Hotel". He was asked by a person named Shaykh Zia, whose last name we cannot say; he might be a *wali* or from the *'abdāl*, a substitute. The Prophet ﷺ said, "If you are lost in a desert or afraid in a forest, call upon the *'abdāl* of Sham and they will come and support you!"

Arrogance Generates a Putrid Smell

Do you think the *'abdāl* of Sham are sitting, not doing anything? Once Grandshaykh 'AbdAllāh al-Fa'iz ad-Daghestani ق went out from his house in Damascus in a horse-drawn carriage with Shaykh 'Abdul-Wahhab as-Salāhi, towards Shaykh Muhiyuddīn's *maqām* and mosque. Shaykh 'Abdul-Wahhab was very famous and he loved Mawlana Shaykh 'AbdAllāh ق a lot. Suddenly a person appeared and held the horse, looked at Shaykh 'Abdul-Wahhab and asked, "Is he your shaykh or are you his shaykh?" because they were very near in age. What did he reply? What will anyone answer, or what will you say?

Shaykh 'Abdul-Wahhab said, "He is not my shaykh and I am not his shaykh."

Immediately that person disappeared, and Shaykh 'Abdul-Wahhab as-Salāhi ﵀ said to Grandshaykh ق, "O my shaykh! Just now he was here and then he disappeared!"

Grandshaykh said, "Yes, but *awlīyāullāh* cannot carry the bad smell that came from what you said."

Shaykh 'Abdul-Wahhab as-Salāhi ﵀ showed some arrogance by answering, "He is not my shaykh and I am not his shaykh," even though he had another shaykh, and yet from that statement came a bad smell! So what then do you think if you backbite? A bad smell like a cigar or cigarette will come from your mouth, or worse, it might be the (bathroom) smell like when you go to make *wudu*!

Grandshaykh ق related that once the *Ṣaḥābah* ﷺ were praying *Tarawīh* with the Prophet ﷺ and then one time Jibrīl ﷺ didn't descend. The Prophet ﷺ asked him, "Why are you not coming?" and Jibrīl ﷺ said, "I cannot stand the bad smell from the mouths of the *Ṣaḥābah* ﷺ and no angels can stand it, because they ate garlic and onions." They are *Ṣaḥābat an-Nabī* ﷺ, about whom Prophet ﷺ said, "My *Ṣaḥābah* are like the stars: whichever of them you follow, you will be rightly guided."

So what do you think about those who spread false rumors and backbite people? Whoever spreads false rumors (*namīmah*) is the sinner. However, whoever repeats that false rumor because they heard it from someone whom they think is a *mu'min* and so they believe it, they are not the sinner!

اية المنافق ثلاث اذا حدث كذب واذا وعد اخلف واذا اتمن خان

Ayatal-munāfiq thalāth idhā hadatha kadhdhab wa idhā waʿda akhlafa wa idhā utumina khān.

The Prophet ﷺ said, "The signs of the munāfiq, hypocrite, are three: if he speaks he lies; if he promises he breaks it; and, if you entrust him with something he betrays you."

Idhā hadatha kadhdhab, "If he speaks he lies"! *Mashā-Allāh,* here the people are very good, but in the second 'section' they lie and that is why they don't put the camera, because they know they might hit on them and so they keep away; no problem, we don't care. What we care about is love to our shaykh, that's it. Correct?

Allāh ﷻ said:

يَا أَيُّهَا الَّذِينَ آمَنُوا إِن جَاءكُمْ فَاسِقٌ بِنَبَإٍ فَتَبَيَّنُوا أَن تُصِيبُوا قَوْمًا بِجَهَالَةٍ فَتُصْبِحُوا عَلَى مَا فَعَلْتُمْ نَادِمِينَ

Yā ayyuha 'Lladhīna āmanū in ja'akum fāsiqun bi naba'in fa-tabayyinū an tusībū qawman bi-jahālatin fatusbihū ʿalā mā faʿltum nādimīn.

O you who believe! If a corrupt person comes to you with something wrong, ascertain the truth unless you harm people unwittingly and afterwards become full of repentance for what you have done. (Sūrat al-Ḥujurāt, 49:6)

Wa idhā utumina khān, "If you trust him with something secret, he betrays you." For example, he might go to the police and say, "They are a terrorist organization; they want to do this and that (wrong)." Do you have proof? Bring the proof. Is it true or not? Am I lying? (No, *hāsha!*) Put the camera on him (Mawlana Shaykh's grandson); he is good one and that is why they don't like him and they are also afraid from him because he is always here, I am not. One Pakistani who was doing nothing, the first time he came here, they beat him up and the next day someone supported them! *Allāhu Akbar*!

Idhā hadatha kadhdhab, "If he speaks, he lies." *Wa idhā utumina khān*, "If you trust him, he betrays you." *Wa idhā w'adā akhlaf*, "If he promises, he breaks it." He might say to your face, "I am good, I didn't do it, I love you!" but he has two faces, *lahu wajhān*, he, she, them ...

We cannot lie! Grandshaykh ʿAbdAllāh ق told this story to Shaykh ʿAbdal-Wahhab as-Salāhi, and you cannot deny he said it.

We are not Buddhists, as some have said. For fifty years we have been with Mawlana Shaykh; are we Buddhists now? And also regarding the 360 points in the human body about which some have objected, we mentioned the *ḥadīth* of point in the human body and also how we hold our fingers.

So Grandshaykh ʿAbdAllāh ق told Shaykh ʿAbdul-Wahhab ق, "That bad smell came from your mouth."

He replied, "What did I say wrong? I only said, 'He is not my shaykh and I am not his shaykh!'"

Grandshaykh ق said, "What would you have lost had you said, 'He is my shaykh.' That would have a nice smell, but the way you said it created a bad smell."

Awlīyāullāh smell the deeds of their followers! If someone believes he or she is near to the shaykh and they lie, don't believe the shaykh does not smell those bad smells issuing from their mouths! The shaykh doesn't show it because Allāh's Name is "*as-Sattar*," and He veils the mistakes of His servants. *Awlīyāullāh* inherit from that secret. Don't you think *Sulṭān al-Awlīyā* inherits from that? So always he will say, "You are the best one on Earth, the biggest shaykh! You are *wazīr al-Mahdi*," or even, "You are Mahdi!" just to make you happy, because the Prophet ﷺ said:

إن من أحب الأعمال إلى الله إدخال السرور على قلب المؤمن

Inna min ahabba'l-ʿamāl ila-Allāhi idkhāl as-surūr ʿalā qalb al-mu'min. Verily from one of the most beloved actions to Allāh is to give happiness to the heart of the believer.

You have to know Shariʿah, which teaches that to make people happy is from *imān*, so make people happy!

Grandshaykh ق told Shaykh ʿAbdul-Wahhab ق, "I am seeing him, he is there, but you are not seeing him as he veiled himself. He is giving *salāms* and he came to teach you *adab*." How much *adab* we need! That is why we are speaking of the Greatness of the Prophet ﷺ, and I mentioned this to show that *raḥmatullāh* is so huge, that with *ṣalāt ʿalā an-Nabī* ﷺ the Prophet ﷺ will intercede for you!

Before I go back to the story of Shaykh Sharafuddin ق, let me mention this point from the book *Jawāhir al-Maʿaniyy, Jewels of Meanings*:

قال : و من فاته كثرة القيام و الصيام فليشغل نفسه بالصلاة على رسول الله صلى الله عليه و سلم ،

Qāla bʿad al-ʿarifīn billāh, wa man fātahu kathrat al-qiyāma wa 's-siyām, fal-yashgul nafsihi bi's-ṣalāt ʿalā an-Nabī ﷺ.

Some awlīyāullāh said, 'What must a person do if he missed many prayers and many days of fasting in Ramadan? (For sure he has to make them up, but also he has to) always increase ṣalawāt on the Prophet ﷺ."

Prayers are an act of obedience to Allāh ﷻ. The Prophet ﷺ said:

من صلى علي واحدة صلى الله عليه عشرا

Man salla ʿalayya marratan sal-Allāhu bihā ʿalayha ʿashara.

If anyone invokes a blessing on me once, Allāh will grant him ten blessings.

(Bukhari and Muslim)

So do it now: say, "*Allāhumma salli ʿala Sayyīdinā Muḥammad* ﷺ." You just did one *ṣalawāt* and Allāh ﷻ gave you ten, but is our *ṣalawāt* like Allāh's? This point is important:

فإنك لو فعلت في عمرك كل طاعة ثم صلى الله عليك صلاة واحدة رجحت تلك الصلاة الواحدة بكل ما عملت في عمرك كله من جميع الطاعات ،

Fa innaka law fa'lta fī 'umrika kullu ta'at thumma salla Allāhu 'alayka ṣalātan wahidatan wa salla 'ala an-Nabī marratan wahidatan rajihat tilka as-ṣalawāt 'ala kullu 'amalihi.

If you, from the day you were born until the day you died, did all kinds of obligations as ordered by Allāh, and Allāh prayed on you one time, (because you prayed on Sayyīdinā Muḥammad [s]), it will be heavier on the Scale than all your ta'at, obedience, (all your prayers and fasting, Hajj and all his acts of obedience)!

That one *ṣalawāt* will be heavier on the Scale! Why? *Sabab yakthuri 'l-'ajab,* "When you mention the cause you will not be astonished (or question it) because when you make one prayer, Allāh ﷻ makes ten prayers for you. So which is heavier, Allāh's prayers or your *ta'at*? If you were to pray and fast continuously from the Day of Creation to the Day of Resurrection, still Allāh's ten *ṣalawāt* for your one would be heavier than all that worship! That's why *awlīyāullāh,* who understood these secrets, said, "If you missed fasting one Ramadan or any of your prayers, make them up, and even if you made them up, since it is not equal to fasting during the time of Ramadan or praying when the prayer is due to be prayed, that prayer on the Prophet ﷺ will be heavier on the Scale!

He explained:

لأنك تصلي على قدر وسعك، و هو سبحانه يصلي على حسب ربوبيته ،

Li annaka tusalli 'alā qadr wis'ak wa Huwa subḥānahu yusalli 'ala hasab rubūbiyyatah.

When you pray (on the Prophet [s]) it is according to your capacity, but when Allāh ﷻ prays on you it is according to His Greatness as Lord!

When we say "Greatness" *Allāhu Akbar,* we mean there are no limits! Whatever you say of greatness, Allāh ﷻ is above that, He is *Akbar*! So He rewards according to <u>His</u> Greatness. Say, "*Allāhumma salli 'alā Sayyīdinā Muḥammad wa 'alā āli Sayyīdinā Muḥammad!*" You just got ten *ṣalawāt* from Allāh ﷻ, and He will give you mercy according to His Greatness.

If Shaykh 'Abdul-Wahhab Salāhi ؓ had shown humbleness by saying, "He is my shaykh," then Allāh ﷻ would have raised him, but he didn't do that, he didn't accept it. We must have a good smell, not a bad smell, so from today let's say we forgive each other. We are on the Internet, all over the world. Let's forget these (bad) things about each other and forgive each other; let's pray that everyone forgives each other and be good in our respective countries, especially in western countries where, when we obey our countries' laws, we obey Allāh, we obey Prophet ﷺ and when we obey those in authority, we obey Allāh ﷻ!

Love everyone! Show love to non-Muslims and tell them Islam is love, Islam is perfect, *imān* is perfect, *ihsān* is perfect! You (who oppose us) are our brothers in humanity, so may Allāh guide us and you! What is the problem with doing this? Show humbleness. And we say, "May Allāh ﷻ forgive everyone here and may they forgive us and we forgive them." What is the issue? Don't be *munāfiq*! *Idhā hadatha kadhdhab*! "If he speaks, he lies." He might say to you, "Yes, I am your friend, you are my friend, I forgive you, you forgive me," and then we see police coming! *Allāhu Akbar*!

We say, "What happened, why are you coming?"

And they say, "Be careful. We are watching!"

Watch as much as you like! All the world knows us, from presidents to prime ministers, from ministers to normal people, and we don't do anything wrong. Mawlana taught us to love everyone and to be humble with everyone!

Look at the story of Shaykh Zia and Shaykh Sharafuddin ad-Daghestani ق, who was staying at Hotel Massarat in Turkey, which I don't know if it still exists or not.

Shaykh Zia asked him, "How are you going to die?"

What kind of question is that? Maybe he wanted to get a secret from Shaykh Sharafuddin ق by which Allāh ﷻ will forgive us and forgive everyone.

Shaykh Sharafuddin ق said, "Is that an important question to you, how I will die?"

He said, "No my shaykh, but it came to my heart to ask it."

That is why you should not speak whatever comes to your heart as it is against the *adab* of *ṭarīqah* and inappropriate! Don't dump out everything that comes to your heart. *Awlīyāullāh* say that is craziness, especially if you whisper such things to others. What is the purpose? First check if it is bad, or will it create a problem or bad situation; ask yourself will repeating it be *ghībah* or *namīmah*, or will it be a good question? For example, you may want to ask your shaykh, "How am I going to make *ṣalawāt* on the Prophet ﷺ?" Don't even ask that; wait until he tells you. Also, your shaykh taught you how to make *ṣalawāt* in the *awrād* book, so don't ask; in *ṭarīqah* there are no questions! The Prophet ﷺ never asked Allāh ﷻ one question in all of the Holy Qur'an. If you look in the entire Holy Qur'an, you will not find any question from the Holy Prophet ﷺ; there are only questions from Sayyīdinā Musa ؑ.

Shaykh Sharafuddin ق answered, "I will die when there is an invasion from Armenia, and there will be too much oppression at that time." He saw ahead (in the future) that Armenian forces would enter Safar Barlik. I heard from Grandshaykh ق that many scholars were executed then and there was so much oppression.

Shaykh Zia's Du`a

With sincerity, Shaykh Zia said, "O Allāh! Take that difficulty from the invasion of the Armenians away from us and spare the life of my shaykh!" He did not say that in front of Shaykh Sharafuddin ق, but rather in private when he was at home.

The next day, Shaykh Sharafuddin ق said to him, "O Shaykh Zia! What have you been doing all night, were you praying? Your prayer has been accepted, and that difficulty has been taken from me and you will suffer instead of me and you will die *shahīd*, a martyr!"

Many people's prayers are accepted ahead of time. Yesterday I heard from someone very close to His Highness, Raja Ashman, that one week before he died he asked, "May Allāh spare my shaykh's life and I give my life in his place!" His personal assistant overheard that. When love overtakes one's heart, all else is finished, no boundaries remain, and Allāh ﷻ accepts.

Eight years after that incident in Hotel Massarat, the Armenians and Greeks entered Rashadiyya, which today is known as Gunekoy, where Shaykh Sharafuddin's *maqām* and *zawiya* are located on top of the mountain, along with the *maqām* of Shaykh Abu Muḥammad al-Madani of the Naqshbandi Golden Chain. As soon as they entered, Zia Effendi was shot and he died a martyr; he gave the remainder of his life to Shaykh Sharafuddin ad-Daghestani ق, whose prediction came to pass.

So can anyone give his life to someone else, to spare their life? Can the shaykh give his life to his *murīd*; can a *murīd* give his life to his shaykh; can anyone give the remainder of his life to spare the life of someone he loves? The answer is yes. That is why the Ṣaḥābah ؇ said, *fidāk nafsī ummī wa abī yā Rasūlullāh*, "Take my life and that of our mother and father (and give them to you) *yā Rasūlullāh!*"

I quote from *Jawāhir al-Maʿaniyy, Jewels of Meanings* by Abdul-Wahhab ash-Shaʿrānī ؇, page 144:

> What is the best *dhikrullāh* and the best way to get rewards? It is *ṣalāt ʿalā rasūlillāh*, to praise the Prophet ﷺ. Everyone is going to die and you want to die peacefully, so make *ṣalāt* on the Prophet ﷺ if you want to die with paradises and rewards and *hur ul-ʿayn*. [We mentioned that shaykh Qassim ؇ saw *hur ul-ʿayn* and Paradise, but he turned away from that and looked to his shaykh. If you always want your last vision to be your shaykh, make *ṣalawāt* on the Prophet ﷺ!] That is what can *mutakaffila*, sponsor you from Allāh ﷻ; making *ṣalawāt* will sponsor you in whatever you ask from Allāh! In *dunya* and *Akhirah*, that *ṣalawāt* will be supporting you in front of Allāh ﷻ!

If you need something to come to you, make *ṣalawāt*! And who will use it the most will be one of the *awlīyāullāh* whom Allāh has chosen.

We will stop here and continue next time with the story of how Mawlana Khalid al-Baghdadi ق spared his life for others.

May Allāh ﷻ forgive us and may Allāh ﷻ bless us.

Wa min Allāhi 't-tawfiq, bi ḥurmati 'l-ḥabīb, bi ḥurmati 'l-Fātiḥah.

And with Allāh is success. For the sake of the Beloved, for his sake we recite the opening chapter of Holy Qur'an.

Proof of the Shaykh Giving His Life to Others

A'ūdhu billāhi min ash-Shayṭāni 'r-rajīm. Bismillāhi' r-Raḥmāni 'r-Raḥīm.
Nawaytu 'l-arbā'īn, nawaytu 'l-'itikāf, nawaytu'l-khalwah, nawaytu 'l-'uzlah,
nawaytu 'r-riyāḍa, nawaytu 's-sulūk, lillāhi Ta'alā fī hādhā 'l-masjid.
Atī'ūllāha wa atī'ū 'r-Rasūla wa ūlī 'l-amri minkum.
Obey Allāh, obey the Prophet, and obey those in authority among you. (4:59)

Dastūr, madad yā Sulṭān al-Awlīyā, Mawlana Shaykh Nazim al-Haqqani ق.
Dastūr, madad yā Sulṭān al-Awlīyā, Mawlana Shaykh 'AbdAllāh ad-Daghestani ق.

First of all, we ask *madad* from Mawlana Shaykh Nazim to send us some support, because without his support none of us can get any kind of inspiration. But with Mawlana Shaykh Nazim's support, everyone will have different inspirations that respond to his heart.

Now you have electricity that comes from the main line that is 360 volts, but they put a transformer to bring it down to 220 volts because the electric system in the *masjid* or house cannot take 360 volts and will explode. Energy comes according to the capacity of each person; some take only 110 volts. To everyone Allāh ﷻ gave a different understanding and way of thinking, and as long as everyone's understanding is in the direction of Islamic Shari'ah, of *haqiqah*, the Islamic way, then *alḥamdulillāh*, that is the best.

It is like driving on Germany's Autobahn. How fast do you go? Perhaps 120 kph, but there are some signs saying, "Slow Down," and these are exits. Shayṭan has many exits on our Autobahn toward love of Allāh ﷻ, love of the Prophet ﷺ and love of *awlīyāullāh*, and at any moment Shayṭan can play with us to make us exit. If he played with Sayyīdina Adam ؏, can't he play with you? So he can lead you out of the main way, off the Autobahn of the Gnostic's way. Gnosticism is *ma'arifatullāh* so any *'arif billāh*, Gnostic, is also on an Autobahn seeking the journey to Allāh, and Shayṭan can mislead them to an exit. None of you come here for any purpose other than love of Mawlana Shaykh Nazim ق, but here the exits are also too many!

So on the Autobahn, when you travel 30, 50, 70 kilometers, you see a rest house on the right or left side with restaurants, coffee and tea shops, quick marts and petrol stations. You exit there to refuel your vehicle, to eat food and then continue on the Autobahn, but if you exit before the rest house, you lose that piece of Paradise that is on *Sirāt al-Mustaqīm,* where you find a lot of benefit. There are a lot of places with gardens on that Autobahn, but if you exit, *thumma āmanū, thumma kafarū*:

إِنَّ الَّذِينَ آمَنُوا ثُمَّ كَفَرُوا ثُمَّ آمَنُوا ثُمَّ كَفَرُوا

Inna alladhīna āmanū thumma kafarū thumma āmanū thumma kafarū. Those who believe then reject faith, then believe (again) and (again) reject faith. (Sūrat an-Nisa, 4:137)

Grandshaykh ق explained this, "One day they are in *āmanū,* belief, then *thumma kafarū,* they make mistakes. To keep on the right way we must show love to Allāh ﷻ, love to the Prophet ﷺ and love to *awlīyāullāh.*

أَطِيعُوا اللَّهَ وَأَطِيعُوا الرَّسُولَ وَأُوْلِي الأَمْرِ مِنكُمْ

Atīʿūllāha wa atīʿū 'r-Rasūla wa ūlī 'l-amri minkum.

Obey Allāh, obey the Prophet, and obey those in authority among you.

(Sūrat an-Nisa, 4:59)

وَمَا آتَاكُمُ الرَّسُولُ فَخُذُوهُ وَمَا نَهَاكُمْ عَنْهُ فَانتَهُوا

Mā atākumu 'r-rasūlu fa-khudhūhu wa mā nahākum ʿanhu fantahū.

Take what the Messenger assigns to you, and deny yourselves that which he withholds from you. (Sūrat al-Hashr, 59:7)

We have explained this as Allāh ﷻ telling us to take whatever the Prophet gave us. Don't say, "No, later," as that will benefit us in *dunya* and *Akhirah.* Yesterday we spoke about the Greatness of Prophet ﷺ and the importance of *ṣalawāt.* Today we will speak on the benefits of making *ṣalawāt* and how one can give his life for the love of Prophet ﷺ, because it is easy to love a *wali* but very difficult to love his followers. Here we see how much the *wali* wants you to love his *murīds* and for all *murīds* to accept each other. Also, Prophet ﷺ wants us to benefit as much as we can from his love.

In the book *Jawahir al-Maʿani,* Imam ash-Shaʿrānī ق wrote that the biggest *dhikrullāh* and the greatest benefit of it is that peacefulness comes to the heart.

Verses of Holy Qur'an about Dhikrullah

الَّذِينَ آمَنُوا وَتَطْمَئِنُّ قُلُوبُهُم بِذِكْرِ اللَّهِ أَلاَ بِذِكْرِ اللَّهِ تَطْمَئِنُّ الْقُلُوبُ

Alladhīna āmanū wa tatmainna qulūbuhum bi dhikri 'Llāhi alā bi dhikri 'Llāhi tatma'inn al-qulūb.

Those who believe and whose hearts find tranquility in the remembrance of God! Verily, in the remembrance of God do hearts find tranquility.

(Sūrat ar-Raʿad, 13:28)

الَّذِينَ يَذْكُرُونَ اللَّهَ قِيَامًا وَقُعُودًا وَعَلَىَ جُنُوبِهِمْ وَيَتَفَكَّرُونَ فِي خَلْقِ السَّمَاوَاتِ وَالأَرْضِ رَبَّنَا مَا خَلَقْتَ هَذا بَاطِلاً سُبْحَانَكَ فَقِنَا عَذَابَ النَّارِ

Alladhīna yadhkurūnullāha qiyamān wa quʿūdan wa ʿalā junūbihim wa yattafakkarūna fī khalqi 's-samāwāti wa 'l-ardi rabbanā mā khalaqta hadhā bātilan subḥānaka fa qinā ʿadhāba 'n-nār.

Those who remember Allāh (always, and in prayers) standing, sitting, and lying down on their sides, and think deeply about the Creation of the Heavens and the Earth, (saying) "Our Lord! You have not created (all) this without purpose! Glory to You! Give us salvation from the torment of the Fire."

(Sūrat Āli 'Imrān, 3:191)

يَا أَيُّهَا الَّذِينَ آمَنُوا اذْكُرُوا اللَّهَ ذِكْرًا كَثِيرًا

Yā ayyuha 'Lladhīna āmanū 'dhkurullāh dhikrun kathīra.

O you who believe! Celebrate the praises of Allāh, and do this often.

(Sūrat al-ʿAhzab, 33:41)

There are so many verses of the Holy Qur'an on *dhikr,* and more than 100 *ayāhs* emphasize the importance of the heart and how to fix it. Allāh ﷻ

mentioned the heart in particular, as there are so many *ayāhs* about it. So when the heart is in love, one will mention the name of whom he loves. Nowadays, Mawlana Shaykh Nazim ق speaks mostly of Sham, because he is so much in love with it, and sometimes he even cries for Sham, because he knows Grandshaykh said:

أوله شام آخره شام

Awwalahu shām Akhirahu shām.

The beginning of it is Sham and the end of it is Sham.

I heard Grandshaykh ق say many times that on Monday, Thursday and Friday nights all *awlīyāullāh* are present with the Prophet ﷺ on Jabal Qasiyoun! Also, Grandshaykh ق said Allāh ﷻ has moved the bodies of all prophets except Sayyīdinā Muḥammad ﷺ to Jabal Qasiyoun; they are all there! More than that, he said, "There are only *mu'mins* in the cemeteries of Sham, because *mu'min* are brought by angels to replace the others." So therefore Sham is clean. Due to their love, *awlīyāullāh* have always had that affection and attraction to Sham.

If you love me, show it, and if I love you, I will show it. We are not making multiple lectures on the topic of love and then you don't show love to anyone (apply this knowledge). Our lectures are not for 'domestic consumption'! Don't say, "I only will hear it." No! *Awlīyāullāh* say, "I love you!" and they mean it.

In *Jawāhir al-Maʿaniyy*, Imam ash-Shaʿrānī said, "The best *dhikr* you can do as a human being and get benefit from it is *ṣalawāt* on the Prophet ﷺ, and it must be with the presence of heart."

We previously explained that he asked the Prophet ﷺ in the dream, "If I make *ṣalawāt* on the Prophet ﷺ, is it necessary for my heart to be present?" And the Prophet ﷺ said, "No, even without presence Allāh will reward one *ṣalawāt* with ten of His Own. And if you do it with presence, Allāh will reward you with what no one knows!" And he said the best of *dhikr* and *afdāl fā'ida*, rewards and benefit, is to do *ṣalawāt* on the Prophet ﷺ with the presence of the heart.

Also, he said the benefit of *ṣalawāt* on Prophet ﷺ is that it will take responsibility for you, *mutakafilan*, it will support you and give you the feeling that you are supported for all your problems in *dunya* and *Akhirah.*

So why do people come and complain? This one want this, that one wants that, this one is ill, that one needs money: sit and make *ṣalawāt!* Then you will see Allāh ﷻ will send people to help you.

I know Mawlana Shaykh Nazim more than everyone, sorry to say. We used to eat together from one plate, and Hajjah Anne ق used to cook and *mashā-Allāh* the fifteen of us sat in his house and enjoyed the meal. They made soup every day, which we ate with bread and it was enough to feed any number of guests! Why? Because the love of Prophet ﷺ is in the heart of Mawlana Shaykh Nazim ق and Hajjah Anne ق never made food without *wudu*. Now most people cook without *wudu*.

Grandshaykh ق had a small hallway and we sat there. One door led to his bedroom, one to his living room where he sometimes sat with people, and one door led to the kitchen. He put a small plate in that hallway, which fed eight-to-ten people maximum. We sat on our knees, which is *adab*, and ate from the same plate. Once we sat there eating with him and he said, "*Yā Sayyidī! Yā Rasūlullāh! Yā Shafiʿi al-Mudhnibīn! unzhur ilaynā!* Look at us! See us! Visit us!" Then he turned suddenly to look at the wall just behind him and said, "The wall is gone and the Prophet is there looking at us!" As I was sitting next to Grandshaykh, immediately I kissed the wall and Grandshaykh said, "You kissed the Prophet ﷺ!"

These are the experiences of *awlīyāullāh,* and you don't know how valuable Mawlana Shaykh Nazim's presence is and how valuable is the presence of *awlīyāullāh* among the *ummah.* You don't know who sits with them and that is why you must keep *adab.* He said so many times not to approach the Sultan, because that is like approaching fire! Don't think you are familiar with the shaykh, and speak with him as if you are speaking with an elderly person. No, you have to be with complete *adab* with the shaykh and listen to him.

Therefore, if you make *ṣalawāt* on the Prophet ﷺ, it will give you support for all your problems in *dunya* and in *Akhirah,* taking care of them immediately! And whoever uses *ṣalawāt* on the Prophet ﷺ excessively, like in *khalwah* when we are ordered to complete 24,000 *ṣalawāt* daily, he will be of the highest level of the chosen people! This is in *Jawāhir al-Maʿaniyy,* page 144, Volume 1. I'm not bringing something unverified.

In this book it also says, *daf'an wa jalban 'an kulli shay*, "They push away anything that might harm you, and anything that will benefit you they bring to you."

As we read yesterday, Shaykh Sharafuddin ad-Daghestani ق was in Istanbul in the Massarat Hotel and Shaykh Zia asked him, "How do you expect to die?"

Shaykh Sharafuddin ق said, "What kind of question is this?"

He answered, "*Yā* Shaykh, I want to know how long you are going to live."

Shaykh Sharafuddin ق said, "I will die when the Armenians invade; that will be when I take my last breath. Why are you asking that?"

Shaykh Zia said, "I want to give my life to you and I will exchange it for your life."

Shaykh Sharafuddin ad-Daghestani ق said, "Don't say that!" But he insisted, then Shaykh Sharafuddin ق said, "Allāh is accepting this from you."

Eight years later the Armenians invaded Rashadiyya, which is now named Gunekoy, and the first person they shot and killed was Shaykh Zia. Shaykh Sharafuddin ق said, "He gave me his life and he took my life." Why? Shaykh Zia was always in *ṣalawāt* out of love for Prophet ﷺ and his shaykh, and *dafa'n wa jalban,* he prevented the killing of his shaykh and put it on himself, although his shaykh was the *Sulṭān al-Awlīyā* of his time! So don't say there is no such thing in Shari'ah! We have previously explained three examples of this:

1. Sayyīdinā Adam ؑ and Sayyīdinā Dawūd ؑ;
2. Shaykh Qassim and his shaykh, 'Ubaydullāh al-Aḥrar ق;
3. Shaykh Sharafuddin ad-Daghestani ق and Shaykh Zia ق.

The fourth example is of Sayyīdinā Khalid al-Baghdadi ق of the Naqshbandi Golden Chain. The history of the black plague that spread in Damascus (1348-1351). Is well known. Shaykh Khalid ق went from Baghdad to India and took *ṭarīqah* from Shaykh Jan-i-Janan Mazhar and then he brought it to Damascus, where it spread. He resided in Jabal Qasiyoun at the mountaintop.

The Prophet ﷺ said to him, "*Yā* Khalid! People will not come to you here so go down to the market every day and ask how much people earn for the day and give it to them and send them up."

So he went to the market and asked, "How much money do you take for one day of work?"

They answered, "Ten dinars."

"Alright, I will pay you ten dinars, but you have to go up to the *zāwīya,* that is your work," and he collected ten people and sent them to the *zāwīya* on the mountain.

So *awlīyāullāh* inherit from the Prophet ﷺ and give out whatever they inherit to their followers. After one year people came by themselves to the *zāwīya* of Sayyīdinā Khalid ق, although he had stopped giving them money. So what about Mawlana Shaykh, will he not be giving? He is giving and Allāh ﷻ is giving, so no one leaves here empty-handed!

As written in the book *Hadāiq al-Wardiyya* by Muḥammad Khani, one night Shaykh Khalid ق entered his house and called his family so he could advise them. Listen, he "called his family," and on Monday evening, when Mawlana Shaykh Nazim got sick and I had not arrived yet, didn't Mawlana Shaykh "call his family" to his room and say to them, "This is my will. I am going!" Did he say that or not, is it correct?

(Sultan's grandson: *Yes, it is*).

So Sayyīdinā Khalid al-Baghdadi ق entered his house and called his whole family, just like Mawlana Shaykh did. It is the same and I am not inventing it, it is in *Hadāiq al-Wardiyya.* He advised them that he was going to die on Friday, so they stayed with him all night. Before *Fajr* he got up to pray *tahajjud* and he was very sick, since the whole city of Damascus was contaminated by the plague. He got up, made ablution and prayed for a while, then he entered his room and said that no one had permission to enter his room except those that he ordered. Did Mawlana Shaykh Nazim say the same thing or not, specifically, "I don't want anyone to enter my room without permission."

(Sultan's grandson: *Yes, correct.*)

And Shaykh Khalid said, "No one may enter my room except by permission," perhaps because the Prophet ﷺ or the *awlīyāullāh* were spiritually present and it would not be good *adab*. When Grandshaykh ق was in Lebanon for his operation forty days before he passed, we collected Mawlana Shaykh Nazim from the airport and brought him to see Grandshaykh ق, who said, "I don't want anyone to be here except Shaykh Nazim." Shaykh Adnan and I were troublemakers in those days, so we looked through the window and saw Mawlana Shaykh Nazim holding Grandshaykh's hand; Mawlana Shaykh was trembling and that went on for half-an-hour. When we knew it was over, we knocked on the door and he let us in and said, "That secret is passed." So they don't want anyone in the room who is not perfect, as in every moment of their life they are perfect and their whole life is perfect.

Shaykh Khalid ق said, "No one may enter my room except those whom I order to do so," then he lay on his right side facing the *qiblah* and said, "I am carrying all the plague which has descended on Damascus." How many times has Mawlana Shaykh Nazim said, "I am carrying the *murīds*," or, "I am carrying the whole *ummah*. The Prophet ﷺ is giving me power to bring *bātil* down and bring *haqq* up." All *awlīyāullāh* are similar.

Shaykh Khalid al-Baghdadi ق raised his hand and prayed. *Allāhu Akbar!* Look at what he said in his prayer, because he wanted to remove that difficulty from everyone. Although his life was meant to be longer, he prayed, "Whoever the plague touches, let it strike me instead!" It meant that he asked, "*Yā Rabb!* I give my life so you may take away death from anyone who would be struck by the plague. I will take that from them and I give my life to them." This is different from Mawlana Qassim, the *murīd* who gave his own life to the shaykh.

In the case of Shaykh Sharafuddin ad-Daghestani ق, the *murīd* gave to the shaykh, but in the case of Mawlana Khalid al-Baghdadi ق, the shaykh is giving to the *murīd*. He said, "Let it strike me instead and spare everyone in Sham who would die." He said that and he was praying inside the locked room.

On Thursday, all 299 of his *khalifahs* entered his room, including Sayyīdinā Isma'īl an-Narānī ق and Sayyīdinā Isma'īl ash-Shirwani ق, and they asked him, "How are you feeling?"

He said, "Allāh has answered my prayer!"

What was his prayer? That anyone who was to be struck by the plague be given life and for it to strike him. So, can *awlīyāullāh* extend life? Yes, when they ask Allāh ﷻ! What is the *du'a* of *Laylat al-Bara'ah*? How many times have we read that *du'a*; don't we read the second *Sūrah YaSīn* with the intention for Allāh to extend our lives? Is that not from the *du'a* of *Laylat al-Bara'ah*, asking Allāh ﷻ to stretch our life? Yes, that is correct, as Allāh ﷻ said in the Holy Qur'an:

> *Wa li-kulli ummatin ajalun fa idhā jā ajaluhum lā yastākhirūna sa'atan wa lā yastaqdimūn.*
>
> *And for all people a term has been set and when their time has come, they can neither delay it by a single moment nor can they hasten it.*
>
> (Sūrat al-A'rāf, 7:34)

But in another *ayah*, Allāh ﷻ says:

> يَمْحُو اللَّهُ مَا يَشَاءُ وَيُثْبِتُ وَعِندَهُ أُمُّ الْكِتَابِ
>
> *Yamhullāha mā yashā wa yuthbitu wa 'indahu ummu 'l-kitāb.*
> *Allāh will erase or confirm whatever He likes and with Him is the Mother of Books.* (Sūrat ar-Ra'd, 13:39)

The *du'a* of a *wali* can bring a change, just as the *du'a* of the Prophet ﷺ will send the whole *ummah* to Paradise! Sayyīdinā Khalid al-Baghdadi ق said, "Allāh ﷻ has answered my prayer. I will take all the plague from the people of Sham and I alone will die on Friday and after they can bury me and everything will be okay." Shaykh Isma'īl an-Narānī ق, his *khalifah* who served him, lived only seven days after Shaykh Khalid and died from the plague; because of his love for his shaykh, he could not live without him!

They offered Shaykh Khalid ق water, but he refused and said, "I left this world behind to meet my Lord." He meant, after Allāh ﷻ accepted his *du'a*, he did not want anything from *dunya*, no food or water. "I have accepted to carry the plague and relieve those in Sham who are infected. I will pass on Friday." His *janāhak* was on Friday and millions of people attended and were cured, which is another story, but in this case the shaykh spared the lives of *murīds*, while in the other case the *murīd* spared his shaykh's life. Also, it is mentioned in the *ḥadīth* of Sayyīdinā Adam ﷺ that he gave forty years of his life to Sayyīdinā Dawūd ﷺ.

Benefits of Making Salawat on the Prophet

Now we will continue with the explanation of some of *fawā'id ṣalawāt 'alā ar-rasūl*, the benefits of *ṣalawāt* on the Prophet ﷺ. I counted 39 of them, but we will not discuss all of them now, we will leave that for next time. However, there is one *ḥadīth* in this book, *Hadāiq al-Wardiyya* that I will mention. (Also appears in *Dalā'il al-Khayrāt* of Imam al-Jazuli in the chapter, "The Benefit of Requesting Blessings upon the Prophet.")

جعل وكما ذكر في كشف الغمة كان صلى الله عليه وسلم يقول من صلى على تعظيما لحقي الله عز وجل من تلك الكلمة ملكا له جناحان جناح في المشرق وجناح في المغرب ورجلاه في تخوم الأرض وعنقه ملتوي تحت العرش يقول الله عز وجل صلى على عبدي كما صلى على نبيي فهو يصلى عليه إلى يوم القيامة

> *Man salla 'alayya ta'zhīman li-haqqī ja'ala Allāhu 'azza wa jall min tilka'l-kalamati malakan lahu janāhun fi 'l-mashriq wa janāhun fi 'l-maghrib wa rijlāhu fi takhūm al-ard wa 'anaqahu multawiyyan taht al-'arsh. Yaqūlullāhu 'azza wa jall salli 'alā 'abdī kamā salla 'ala nabiyyī fa-huwa yusallī 'alayhi ila yawm al-qiyāmat.*

'Abdur Raḥman ibn 'Awf ؓ narrated that the Prophet ﷺ said:

> *Whenever someone asks for blessings upon me, magnifying my rights and station, Allāh ﷻ creates from his words an angel with wings stretching from the east to the west with feet connected to the nethermost part of the seventh earth and a neck bent beneath the Throne. Allāh ﷻ says to him, "Bless My slave as he asks for blessings upon My Prophet," and thereupon the angel will bless him until the Day of Resurrection.*

It is not the east we see on this Earth, but rather it is the east of the entire universe, which is always moving westward, as verified in physics: the universe is moving west, not just one galaxy but all 6,000 galaxies. Each galaxy has 80 billion stars and all are moving in a vacuum to the west. That is why Allāh ﷻ mentioned in different verses of Holy Qur'an, "*mashriq wa 'l-maghrib*," or, "*mashriqayni wa 'l-maghribayn*," or, "*mashāriq wa maghārib*." That whole universe is moving from east to west at the speed of light, 300,000 km per second. Where it is going no one knows, but it is moving in a vacuum with no gravity. *Subḥān-Allāh!*

The Prophet ﷺ said from that *ṣalawāt*, Allāh ﷻ will create an angel with one wing in the east that is moving, and one wing in the west that also keeps moving. That means it is reaching both ends of what Allāh said:

بَدِيعُ السَّمَاوَاتِ وَالأَرْضِ وَإِذَا قَضَى أَمْرًا فَإِنَّمَا يَقُولُ لَهُ كُن فَيَكُونُ

Badīʿu 's-samāwāti wa 'l-ardi wa idhā qadā amran fa innamā yaqūlu lahu kun fa-yakūn.

He is the Originator of the Heavens and the Earth and when He wills a thing to be, He but says unto it, "Be" and it is. (Sūrat al-Baqara, 2:117)

Allāh ﷻ said, *"Kun faya kūn,"* which means He commands into existence all that is and all that will be, and the angels are in *ṣalawāt* as they are ordered. Where is that east and that west? It means that wing is moving as well, expanding more and more, like a child whose small arms grow until they are the size of an adult's. One of the angel's wings is in the east and one is in the west and his two legs are rooted in the Earth. "Earth" here is not our Earth; there are seven earths within this solar system that are like ours and nearby, but scientists cannot find them. His feet are rooted in the Earth and his head is not erect because he is so tall, so it is bowed under the Throne. This is all from *ṣalawāt* on the Prophet ﷺ!

Allāh ﷻ says to that angel, "Make *ṣalawāt* on My servant who is making *ṣalawāt* on My Prophet and as he praised My Prophet, O angel, you praise him!" There is a big meaning in this. *Allāhu Akbar!* Can we understand that? No, it is beyond our mind. And that is from just one *ṣalawāt*! If you make *ṣalawāt* two times, there are two angels and if you say it 100 times you have 100 angels, and so on. None of the angels recite the same, each one is reciting a different *ṣalawāt* on Prophet ﷺ as Allāh ﷻ does not use copy machines! He creates millions of angels for one person making *ṣalawāt* on the Prophet ﷺ! That is why *awlīyāullāh* emphasize the reality of making *ṣalawāt*; for even one *ṣalawāt*, *fa huwa yusalli ilā Yawm al-Qiyāmah,* and that angel will be praying on your behalf until the Day of Judgment!

May Allāh ﷻ forgive us and may Allāh bless us. I am sorry for any mistake in delivering this lecture, but it is about the Greatness of Sayyīdinā Muḥammad ﷺ and of *awlīyāullāh* who inherit from the Prophet ﷺ. We are helpless, we are sinners, we are weak and we ask in every moment that Allāh ﷻ forgives us and forgives everyone.

May Allāh ﷻ forgive us and may Allāh ﷻ bless us.

Wa min Allāhi 't-tawfiq, bi ḥurmati 'l-ḥabīb, bi ḥurmati 'l-Fātiḥah.

And with Allāh is success. For the sake of the Beloved, for his sake we recite the opening chapter of Holy Qur'an.

Introduction to Sultan adh-Dhikr

Aʿūdhu billāhi min ash-Shayṭāni 'r-rajīm. Bismillāhi' r-Raḥmāni 'r-Raḥīm.
Nawaytu 'l-arbāʿīn, nawaytu 'l-ʿitikāf, nawaytu'l-khalwah, nawaytu 'l-ʿuzlah,
nawaytu 'r-riyāḍa, nawaytu 's-sulūk, lillāhi Taʿalā fī hādhā 'l-masjid.
Atīʿūllāha wa atīʿū 'r-Rasūla wa ūlī 'l-amri minkum.
Obey Allāh, obey the Prophet, and obey those in authority among you. (4:59)

Dastūr, madad yā Sulṭān al-Awlīyā, Mawlana Shaykh Nazim al-Haqqani ق.
Dastūr, madad yā Sulṭān al-Awlīyā, Mawlana Shaykh ʿAbdAllāh ad-Daghestani ق.

As-salāmu ʿalaykum wa raḥmatullāhi wa barakatuh. Yesterday we completed clarification of a series of different matters, some issues that had recently been a little misunderstood, and we spoke in the previous lectures about the Greatness of the Prophet ﷺ, which we were going to explain further, and we mentioned yesterday that there are thirty-nine different categories of benefits on Muslims from reciting *ṣalawāt* on the Prophet ﷺ.

But first I would like to say that the Holy Qur'an is Allāh's ﷻ Ancient Words, and that is why *Ahlu 's-Sunnah wa 'l-Jamaʿah* and most of the Muslims, other than Imam az-Zamaskhari and some scholars [of other Muslim doctrines], say that the Holy Qur'an is *ghayra makhlūq,* not created. Just as Allāh's Beautiful Names and Attributes describe the Essence of Allāh, the Holy Qur'an is Allāh's Ancient Words and it is not created as an entity; the Holy Qur'an is Allāh's Words revealed to the Prophet ﷺ. Most scholars believe that and it is one of the obligations to be Muslim.

The reason I am bringing this up is to relate a story which happened in the time of Sayyīdinā Musa ؑ. Prophets like to travel and *awlīyāullāh* inherit from them, so they also travel. That is why we recorded in the book *Classical Islam and the Naqshbandi Sufi Way* that Mawlana Shaykh Nazim's, may Allāh ﷻ give him *shifaʿa,* whole life has been a journey of traveling by body or by soul, as *awlīyāullāh* can also travel by soul. Many people have seen him, although physically he may not have moved, but in spirit he went somewhere and people who know him have seen him and there are a lot of examples of that.

One example that I can mention took place in the early 1980s when the Prime Minister of Lebanon, along with the governor of the city, came to visit Mawlana Shaykh Nazim, who normally stayed with me in Lebanon. They invited Mawlana Shaykh to go to *Hajj*, and everyone knows this story. Mawlana said, "This year I am busy and cannot go." Although he made *Hajj* physically twenty-seven times and I also heard that he made *Hajj* forty times, that year he said, "I am not going." He was in our home in Tripoli; after the Israeli invasion of Beirut in 1982 we moved to Tripoli from Beirut. He didn't agree to go with them to *Hajj*, so they left. When you are invited by a prime minister or by the government of *Hijaz*, you will be given special treatment; it will be a very comfortable *Hajj* and you may even go inside the *Ka'bah*, pray there and wash the inside of the *Ka'bah*. But he didn't go, stayed with us.

When the *Hajj* finished, the prime minister and the governor of the city returned, and after one week Mawlana Shaykh said, "Let us go and welcome them back and take gifts for them," because we were very close to that prime minister, whose plane was shot down in the Lebanese war. And he said to Mawlana Shaykh, "*Mashā-Allāh, Yā Sayyidī*! You didn't come with us, but you went with the other group!" We looked at each other and wondered what is he saying. There was another group of politicians from Lebanon that went to *Hajj* separately, and the prime minister and the governor of Tripoli said to us, "*Mashā-Allāh* you liked their invitation more than our invitation, and we had that beautiful conversation around the *Ka'bah* and made that *du'a* behind you." We were shocked, but a *wali* is a *wali*, cannot change. If Allāh ﷻ wants to give *wilayah* to someone, He will give, regardless of their actions.

What about Mawlana Shaykh Nazim ق, someone who spends day and night in *da'wah*, who all his life is bringing people to Islam and *ṭarīqah*? So much so that even his sleep is *da'wah* as he separates from people and goes with his soul to wherever and to whomever Allāh ﷻ takes him! And we see this a lot today on the Internet: people take *baya'* and say, "We saw you, Mawlana!" And they are not seeing him just in dreams, but physically.

We were visiting Madinah, it was one o'clock in the morning, and a man came to us. I told Omar to take a picture quickly, and we were outside the Haram al-Madani, visiting relics of the Prophet ﷺ when one person of *Ahlu 'l-Bayt* came to us. He was two meters tall and I looked at him and he looked at me, and I thought of the description of Sayyīdinā al-Mahdi ﷺ that Grandshaykh ʿAbdAllāh ad-Daghestani ق had given us, that "Sayyīdinā Mahdi is so tall and his hands extend down to his knees, and his hand is so big that you can place eight beans end-to-end across his wrist." He looked like that person.

I looked at that man and said, "I know you."

He said, "Yes, from twenty-five years ago, but I know your shaykh not just from twenty-five years ago but since the Day of *Alastu bi-Rabbikum, "Am I not your Lord?"* on the Day of Promises."

I have his picture and it will attract you. His turban is three times bigger and wider than the normal Naqshbandi turban. This was outside the *Muwājaha* (Holy Grave of the Prophet [s]) near *Jannat al-Baqiʿ*. So *awlīyāullāh* are in motion and their every breath is a motion. I explained to you the *ḥadīth* from Bukhari and Muslim in the book, *Bāb az-Zakāt* about when Allāh ﷻ created Sayyīdinā Adam ﷺ and stroked his back, and drips came. When Allāh ﷻ created Man, He created him with 360 points, and I explained in detail that we are not Buddhist. If Buddhists are taking from what the Prophet ﷺ is saying, they are taking because they see it's perfection. We also mentioned the Prophet ﷺ said there are 360 *mafsal*, points, and that Egyptian doctors studied the human skeleton and found it consists of 360 points as the Prophet ﷺ had said.

Yesterday I was sitting with Mawlana Shaykh ق and he said to me, "Why don't you speak to them about the nine *walis* and the nine points that represent them?" Every point represents a *wali*, as mentioned in *The Naqshband Sufi Way*. Every one of these nine *walis* represent a point in the system of the human body and they are all part of the Golden Chain of whom there are 39 up to today, since you don't count the Prophet ﷺ, but you count from Sayyīdinā Abu Bakr as-Siddiq ﷺ. You may also exclude Sayyīdinā Abu Muḥammad al-Madani ق if you want, as he was not from the Naqshbandi Ṭarīqah, but because he was Shaykh Sharafuddin's uncle, for *barakah* he added him to the *silsilah*. Mawlana Shaykh said these nine *awlīyāullāh* have *Sultan adh-Dhikr*. What is the best *dhikr*?

افضل الذكر لا اله الا الله

Afdalu 'dh-dhikri lā ilāha illa-Llāh.

The best remembrance of Allāh is to say, "There is no god but Allāh."

(Tirmidhi)

And then to say, "*Allāh*," and after that best of *dhikr* is to recite *ṣalawāt* on the Prophet ﷺ. And the best of the best is the Holy Qur'an:

إِنَّا نَحْنُ نَزَّلْنَا الذِّكْرَ وَإِنَّا لَهُ لَحَافِظُونَ

Inna nahnu nazzalna 'dh-dhikr wa inna lahu la-ḥāfizhūn.

Behold! It is We Ourselves Who have bestowed from on high, step by step, this reminder and behold, it is We Who shall truly guard it (from all corruption).

(Sūrat al-Hijr, 15:9)

"We have revealed the dhikr," means the Holy Qur'an and, "We are the One that protects it." Now scholars say this means there will be no changes made to the Book, of course Allāh ﷻ will protect His Book, His Words!

وَمَا يَعْلَمُ تَأْوِيلَهُ إِلاَّ اللّهُ وَالرَّاسِخُونَ فِي الْعِلْمِ يَقُولُونَ آمَنَّا بِهِ كُلٌّ مِّنْ عِندِ رَبِّنَا

Wa mā yaʿlamu tāwīlahu illa-Llāh wa'r-rāsikhūn fi 'l-ʿilmi yaqūlūn āmana bihi. kullun min ʿinda rabbinā.

No one knows the interpretation of the Holy Qur'an except Allāh ﷻ. And those who are firmly grounded in knowledge say: "We believe in the Book; the whole of it is from our Lord. (Sūrah Āli ʿImrān, 3:7)

But *awlīyāullāh* say, "We believe," and that's why Allāh inspires them. That's why you see there are hundreds of *tafsīr* of the Holy Qur'an, which differs from one scholar to another and similarly, the interpretation differs between different *awlīyāullāh*. If Allāh ﷻ is protecting His Holy Words, what is the *Sultan adh-Dhikr*? It is the Holy Qur'an, which is the Sultan of all *dhikr* that Allāh Himself is protecting! And it means He is protecting it in the hearts of *awlīyāullāh* and giving to them realities and secrets according to their capacity they can carry.

So these nine *awlīyāullāh* that Grandshaykh ق mentioned are nine in number, from Sayyīdinā Aba Yazid al-Bistami ق, all the way to

Grandshaykh ʿAbdAllāh ق and to Mawlana Shaykh Nazim ق. And these nine points represent one *wali* on each point. In Naqshbandi Ṭarīqah and other *ṭarīqas* there are seven *latā'if* and there are five levels of the heart: *qalb, sirr, sirr as-sirr, khafā,* and *akhfā.* So Grandshaykh ق said that *Sultan adh-Dhikr* is reading all of the Holy Qur'an with its secret. And Sayyīdinā Bayazid al-Bistami ق was able to read the Holy Qur'an with its secrets only once in his life, because there are 24,000 oceans of knowledge on every letter, and there are almost 350,000 letters in the Holy Qur'an and 6,666 verses, *āyāt al-Qur'an.*

Sayyīdinā Bayazid ق was able to complete the Holy Qur'an in his life, not reading as we read; rather, you read one *juz'* and you finish in thirty days or if you read three then you finish in ten days. When I used to go for *tarawīh* in *Madinat al-Munawarrah,* I used to go late because the imam of the mosque used to read one or one-and-a-half *juz'* every night and finish Holy Qur'an by *Laylat al-Qadr.* And there was another group with Shaykh Abbas, who is Bukhari and Grandshaykh's *murīd* who died at more than a hundred years of age.

I will tell you one story about Hafizh ʿAbbas Qāri from Uzbekistan. He used to slaughter a lamb and feed so many dervishes, and we ate at his *zāwīya.* When he reached seventy years of age, he wanted to marry. His helper brought a lady for him to marry, and when she came to his house she was completely covered from head-to-toe; no one could see anything. He had a small apartment with one room, a bedroom, kitchen and bathroom, and his *dargah* was called *Madrassat ash-Shūna, Waqf il-Bukhariyya,* Trust of the Bukhari People. That lady married him and then she entered her room and never came out until she died twenty-seven years later! There was not even a window in that room. No one saw even one nail of her finger, and she spent twenty-seven years in that room and never came out until the day she died, and we took her to her *janāhak* at *Jannat al-Baqiʿ.* Twenty-seven years! This is an example of who Shaykh ʿAbbas al-Qāri was.

There was one room there in the *dargah,* in which Grandshaykh ق made a seclusion for one year, and Mawlana Shaykh ق made seclusions in the room next to him, one for six months and another for three months, so a total of nine months. After the seclusion, it was the first *Hajj* we went on in 1967, Grandshaykh ق said to Mawlana Shaykh Nazim, "Let them stay in your room where you made seclusion and teach them (Shaykh Adnan and myself) from the secrets of the Naqshbandi Way." One secret was about the nine points. I forgot something: I used to pray *tarawīh* prayers with Shaykh Abbas during Ramadan and we took six hours! Not one-and-a-half hours, but six hours of *tarawīh*. We would finish the entire Holy Qur'an in three days, and some years we finished in five days. Your feet would become numb, you would be unable to stand anymore, and still Shaykh Abbas would be standing like a bird (light as a feather). He was a *wali*, a representative of Grandshaykh ʿAbdAllāh ad-Daghestani ق.

If Shaykh Abbas is like that, then what do you think about *Sulṭān al-Awlīyā*, the one to whom we are connected? Are we lucky, or not? We are very lucky that he doesn't ask us to do anything, since he is carrying everything on his shoulders! In *Ṣalāt* an-Najāt, the responsibility of the shaykh is to take away all the sins of the *murīds* and present them clean to the Prophet ﷺ. Grandshaykh ق used to say, "All *murīds* pass before me one-by-one in five minutes and I take all their difficulties on me, and I present them to the Prophet ﷺ." This secret was passed to Mawlana Shaykh ق through his arm when Grandshaykh ق was in the hospital; he held Shaykh Nazim's arm and poured everything from his heart into him, after which we were given permission to enter the room.

Whatever we say about *awlīyā*, we cannot give them their rights. Whatever we say is like a drop in the ocean. Don't say, "He is sick." Physically he is sick, but spiritually they are lions! Mawlana Shaykh Nazim ق said he is the only *murīd* who made *khalwah* with his shaykh, because usually they don't accept that. He said when Grandshaykh ق made *duʿa* the whole building would shake, much like Sayyīdinā Yusuf al-Hamadani ق, by whose *du'a* the angels of the Throne used to tremble! Allāh ﷻ gave them power that we don't see. They will never stop; even after death they are stronger and stronger, and in their life they are stronger and stronger!

Shaykh Bayazid al-Bistami ق completed the *Sultan adh-Dhikr* once in his lifetime. Shaykh Sharafuddin ق spoke to Turkish scholars who visited him in Rashadiyya, who often said, "You always give importance to ʿAbdAllāh Effendi."

He asked, "Do you want me to tell you where he is putting his feet now, or where he will put his feet on Judgment Day (what his rank is now or on the Day of Judgment)? Where he is putting his feet now, none of the *awlīyāullāh* from all time has entered! And if I tell you what his level will be on Judgment Day, you will not understand what I am saying! ʿAbdAllāh Effendi didn't complete *Sultan adh-Dhikr* once, like Bayazid and other *awlīyāullāh* completed it many more times, but with every breath ʿAbdAllāh Effendi takes he completes *Sultan adh-Dhikr*! Every time he inhales, he completes *Sultan adh-Dhikr* and every time he exhales, he completes *Sultan adh-Dhikr* with that power Allāh ﷻ gave to him! He completes it with all its secret oceans of Realities and knowledges and new information coming out to him!"

Grandshaykh ق was like that for his whole life and he said, "I passed that secret to Shaykh Nazim." So don't underestimate the power of *shuyūkh*!

The Shaykh's Power is not on Our Level

The Prophet ﷺ said:

إنما الأعمال بالنيات, وإنما لكل امرئ ما نوى, فمن كانت هجرته إلى الله ورسوله, فهجرته إلى الله ورسوله, ومن كانت هجرته لدنيا يصيبها أو امرأة ينكحها, فهجرته إلى ما هاجر إليه

Innama al-ʿamālu bi 'n-niyyāt wa innamā li kulli imrin mā nawā. Man kāna hijratuhu ila 'Llāhi wa rasūlihi, fa hijratahu ila mā hājara ilayh, wa man kānat hijratuhu ila dunya yusībuhā aw imrātan yankihuhā fa hijratuhu ila mā hājara ilayh.

Verily actions are by intentions, and for every person is what he intended. So the one whose emigration was to Allāh and His Messenger, then his emigration was to Allāh and His Messenger, and the one whose emigration was for the world to gain from it, or a woman to marry him, then his emigration was to what he made it. (Bukhari and Muslim)

Innama al-ʿamālu bi 'n-niyyāt, "Every action is according to intention." If your intention was good to Allāh ﷻ and His Prophet ﷺ, He knows. If he is coming to this house and to this heavenly, spiritual, angelic *maqām* on Earth from Heaven, his intention has to be clean or else what is the benefit? *Man kāna hijratuhu ila 'Llāhi wa rasūlihi, fa hijratahu ila mā hājara ilayh,* if your intention is to come here for Mawlana Shaykh and the *barakah* that he represents, not for any *dunya* benefit, Allāh knows. *Faman kānat hijratuhu ila dunya yusībuhā aw imrātan yankihuhā,* "If he is making *hijrah* for *dunya* or a desire, or to marry a wife, then he is coming for that purpose." Allāh ﷻ knows his intention.

لو كانت الدنيا تزن عند الله جناح بعوضة لما سقى كافراً منها شربة ماء

Law kānati 'd-dunya tazina ʿindAllāhi janāha baʿūdatan mā saqā kāfirun minhā shurbatu ma'a.

If the value of this dunya weighed the wing of a mosquito, Allāh would never give a cup of water for the unbelievers to drink.

(Tirmidhi's *Sunan*, Ibn Majah's *Sunan*, Bayhaqi in *Shuʿb al-Imān*)

If the value of this *dunya* weighs the wing of mosquito, Allāh will not give one cup of water to an unbeliever, so Allāh knows. Let us clean our hearts and speak the truth; let us not go and put unspoken words into the ears or the mouths or their eyes! Remember the *ayah* in Holy Qur'an:

يَا أَيُّهَا الَّذِينَ آمَنُوا إِن جَاءكُمْ فَاسِقٌ بِنَبَأٍ فَتَبَيَّنُوا أَن تُصِيبُوا قَوْمًا بِجَهَالَةٍ فَتُصْبِحُوا عَلَى مَا فَعَلْتُمْ نَادِمِينَ

Yā ayyuha 'Lladhīna āmanū in ja'akum fāsiqun bi naba'in fa-tabayyinū an tusībū qawman bi-jahālatin fatusbihū ʿalā mā faʿltum nādimīn.

O you who believe! If a corrupt person comes to you with something wrong, ascertain the truth unless you harm people unwittingly and afterwards become full of repentance for what you have done. (Sūrat al-Ḥujurāt, 49:6)

This is especially true here, since this place is *Jannah*, Paradise. It is much like when Iblīs tried to come to Sayyīdinā Adam ﷺ in Paradise disguised as a snake. Don't try to come in a different form. Make *ṣalawāt* on the Prophet ﷺ and that will change what you did; even if you spoke wrongly about someone and put words into the mouth of someone, *istighfār* and *ṣalawāt* will clean that. Make *ṣalawāt* and repent; Allāh ﷻ will take that away.

I ask, would any of you like to eat the raw flesh of his brother, as Allāh ﷻ said in Holy Qur'an?

وَلَا تَجَسَّسُوا وَلَا يَغْتَب بَّعْضُكُم بَعْضًا أَيُحِبُّ أَحَدُكُمْ أَن يَأْكُلَ لَحْمَ أَخِيهِ مَيْتًا فَكَرِهْتُمُوهُ

Wa lā tajasassū wa lā yaghtab bʿadakum bʿadan ayyuhibbu ahadukum an yākula lahma ākhīhi maytan fa-karihtumūh.

And spy not on each other behind their backs. Would any of you like to eat the flesh of his dead brother? No, you would abhor it. (Sūrat al-Ḥujurāt, 49:12)

No, since it would be disgusting to eat the flesh of your dead brother. That is why if someone tells you something about someone else, say, "I don't want to hear it." I never heard Mawlana Shaykh Nazim ق or Grandshaykh ق mention anything about something that occurred even one hour before! When someone came and spoke bad things about others, they said, "I don't want to hear it," because then Shayṭan comes.

May Allāh ﷻ forgive me if I said something wrong and that made them upset, may Allāh forgive them if they said something wrong and made people upset, and may Allāh forgive all of us if we said something wrong and made others upset. *Fātiḥah.*

May Allāh ﷻ forgive us and may Allāh ﷻ bless us.

Wa min Allāhi 't-tawfīq, bi ḥurmati 'l-ḥabīb, bi ḥurmati 'l-Fātiḥah.

And with Allāh is success. For the sake of the Beloved, for his sake we recite the opening chapter of Holy Qur'an.

The Meaning of Allah's Order to "Obey Those in Authority"

Aʿūdhu billāhi min ash-Shayṭāni 'r-rajīm. Bismillāhi' r-Raḥmāni 'r-Raḥīm.
Nawaytu 'l-arbāʿīn, nawaytu 'l-ʿitikāf, nawaytu'l-khalwah, nawaytu 'l-ʿuzlah,
nawaytu 'r-riyāḍa, nawaytu 's-sulūk, lillāhi Taʿalā fī hādhā 'l-masjid.
Atīʿūllāha wa atīʿū 'r-Rasūla wa ūlī 'l-amri minkum.
Obey Allāh, obey the Prophet, and obey those in authority among you. (4:59)

Dastūr, madad yā Sulṭān al-Awlīyā, Mawlana Shaykh Nazim al-Haqqani ق.
Dastūr, madad yā Sulṭān al-Awlīyā, Mawlana Shaykh ʿAbdAllāh ad-Daghestani ق.

There are two meanings of, "in authority". One meaning that is very important, is, "the authority of (spiritual) guides," *Al-Murshidūn al-Iʿzhām,* those who guide us to the right way of Islam, because not everyone is an expert in Shariʿah and *tasawwuf.*

Imam Abu Hanifa ؓ wrote in his book *Al-Hidaya* about his *madhhab,* school of thought, *law lā sannatān la-halaka nuʿman,* "If not for two years, I would have been lost and my *madhhab* would not have been as it should be." It means in those two years he spent in his life what you might spend all your life doing. Like Sayyīdinā Imam Abu Hanifa ؓ, one of the greatest *Imams* whom, whenever Mawlana Shaykh Nazim mentions his name, he calls him *Imam ʿAzham,* "Great Imam." Hundreds of millions follow his *madhhab,* especially in India. Also, some in Arab countries and others follow Imam ash-Shafiʿī ؓ or other *Imams,* and all of the *Imams* go to Prophet ﷺ. Sayyīdinā Imam Abu Hanifa ؓ said, "If not for those two years I spent with a guide who guided me, then all my *madhhab* would have been incomplete because I was inspired by that shaykh, that *Imam* who filled my heart and without him I would have been lost!" That's why you must have an *imam.*

His *imam* was Sayyīdinā Jaʿfar as-Sādiq ق, one of the grandsons of Sayyīdinā ʿAlī ؓ, from the chain of the *aʿimma* of *imams.* Imam Abu Hanifa ؓ said, "In the two years I spent with him, I saved myself and my *madhhab.*"

They can guide us and they are authorities on you. Also, *awlīyāullāh* take from these secrets from *imams,* because the Prophet ﷺ said:

أصحابي كالنجوم بأيهم اقتديتم اهتديتم

Aṣ-ḥābī ka 'n-nujūm bi ayyihim aqtadaytum ahtadaytum.

My Companions are like stars (on a dark night); whichever of them you follow, you will be guided. (Bukhari)

How can you be guided at night with no light or radar? Before technology, in the old times, people were guided by and knew how to find directions by the stars. Prophet ﷺ is telling us, "My Companions are like stars; whichever you follow, you will be guided to me." Some people might say this *ḥadīth* is not strong, although we know there are 32 different grades of *ḥadīth*, but it might be one *Sahābi* heard that from the Prophet ﷺ, and not another one, as not every *ḥadīth* was heard by all the *Ṣaḥābah*. For example, today you are here, but tomorrow you will see different people here, just as yesterday different people were here. So you have to summarize what was said yesterday to inform these new people so they can understand what we are saying today.

So in the time of the Prophet ﷺ, different *Ṣaḥābah* heard different *aḥadīths* from him. Imam Bukhari ؓ collected them, but only put 3000 *ḥadīth* in his *Saḥih al-Bukhari*. Also, Imam Aḥmad ؓ, the most strict of the Four Imams, said, "I memorized 300,000 *aḥadīth* and know which is correct and which is not correct." So you need an *imam,* a Shaykh, an authority.

Imam Malik ؓ said, *man tafaqqaha wa lam yatasawwaf,* "Who studied Shari'ah but not *tasawwuf,* which means good characters and moral excellence. Like today I see so many people pray (so fast, without proper bowing, etc.), although the Prophet ﷺ said, "Don't pray like the pecking of a rooster." Many people pray like that, but it is not accepted, so don't do it! What is the benefit of such a prayer by which we are missing a lot?

Imam Malik ؓ famously said, *man tasawaffa wa lam yatafaqqa faqad tazandaqa, wa man tafaqqaha wa lam yatasawwaf faqad tafassaq, wa man tasawaffa wa tafaqqaha faqad tahaqqaq,* "Whoever studied Sufism without *fiqh* is a heretic, and whoever studied *fiqh* without Sufism is corrupted, and whoever studied Sufism and *fiqh* will find the truth and reality of Islam." That is because such a person may pray and fast but, as the Prophet ﷺ asked the *Ṣaḥābah* ؓ:

"Who is the muflis, bankrupted one?" and they said, "The one with no money." He ﷺ said, "No, it is the one with no ʿamal." They said, "Even if he prayed and fasted?" He ﷺ said, "Even if he prayed and fasted."

Every day he has to audit his deeds of the day, which can only be done by sitting and making *tafakkur,* about which the Prophet ﷺ said:

تفكر ساعة خير من عبادة سبعين سنة

Tafakkarru saʿatin khayrun min ʿibādati sabaʿīn sannah.

To remember Allāh ﷻ for one hour (contemplate or meditate) is better than seventy years of worship.

Also, Allāh ﷻ said in Holy Qur'an:

الَّذِينَ يَذْكُرُونَ اللّهَ قِيَامًا وَقُعُودًا وَعَلَىَ جُنُوبِهِمْ وَيَتَفَكَّرُونَ فِي خَلْقِ السَّمَاوَاتِ وَالأَرْض
رَبَّنَا مَا خَلَقْتَ هَذا بَاطِلاً سُبْحَانَكَ فَقِنَا عَذَابَ النَّارِ

Alladhīna yadhkurūnullāha qiyamān wa quʿūdan wa ʿalā junūbihim wa yattafakkarūna fī khalqi 's-samāwāti wa 'l-ardi rabbanā mā khalaqta hadhā bātilan subḥānaka fa qinā ʿadhāba 'n-nār.

Those who remember Allāh (always, and in prayers) standing, sitting, and lying down on their sides, and think deeply about the Creation of the Heavens and the Earth, (saying) "Our Lord! You have not created (all) this without purpose! Glory to You! Give us salvation from the torment of the Fire."

(Sūrat Āli ʿImrān, 3:191)

So in the *ayāh, Atīʿūllāha wa atīʿū 'r-Rasūla wa ūlī 'l-amri minkum,* "Obey Allāh, obey the Prophet, and obey those in authority among you," there are two types of "*ūlī 'l ʿamr,*" authorities, who should be obeyed.

Two Types of Authority

Imam Malik ؓ said, "Those who study Shariʿah but not diplomacy (learning how to speak with people) are corrupted." Today the whole world is taking diplomacy and moral excellence from Islam and they leave out Shariʿah, but in Islam you must have both! He said, *man tasawwafa wa tafaqqaha faqad tahaqqaq!* "Who studied *tasawwuf* and *fiqh* will find reality."

"Who studied *tasawwuf*" means those who become good people and eliminate their bad characters, especially backbiting. There are many who spread rumors and make *fitna*, not knowing their limits and transgressing them; they pass red lights and don't even care! You don't pass through the red light while on the road because a camera is taking pictures. Aren't there heavenly cameras on your shoulders? Which is better, physical cameras or heavenly cameras? Heavenly cameras record our bad actions with high definition, perfect images! However, Allāh ﷻ has ordered the angels, "Don't record anything until they repent," or, "until they make *wudu* and pray," or, "if they come for *Jumuʿah* prayers," then Allāh ﷻ tells His angels, "Take the good, leave the bad!" Allāh ﷻ knows what we are doing, but He is The Forgiving and The Merciful.

So Imam Malik ؓ is saying, "Whoever studied to become a 'Shariʿah man' and a '*tasawwuf* man,' has found reality." Imam Malik ؓ was not present at the time of Imam Jaʿfar as-Sadiq ق, but Imam Abu Hanifa ؓ was lucky, because he studied directly with Imam Jaʿfar. About this Abu Hanifa ؓ said, "If not for these two years spent with an *imam* from *Ahlu 'l-Bayt*, my eighty years of studying would have been nothing!" How many years have you been spending here with an *imam* from *Ahlu 'l-Bayt*? This is a blessing for us, but it is very dangerous to have bad *adab* in front of them by disrespecting their orders!

Everyone here is ordered only up to the door. Can you go passed the door? Someone else may have an order to go inside. Some may have more, such as to be with the shaykh and his family, they are allowed, but those who think they are higher than his family and send messages saying they are part of his family are making a mistake. You must know your limits! I am not saying something to make you upset, but it's for your benefit as well as ours.

Our ladies want to sit in their father's home without covering their heads. Is this correct? Can you allow yourself to go in while they are uncovered? I am giving this one example, although there are many others than this. We have to be careful! When Mawlana Shaykh says, "This whole place is for women," then that matter is finished and you are not even supposed to stand behind the window with Mawlana Shaykh Nazim! They called me and said, "Mawlana is behind the window come and stand with him!" I said, "No. I want everyone to see only Mawlana Shaykh!" We are nothing, our gaze is to him, nothing else. That is why sitting with the shaykh is like sitting with fire.

Grandshaykh ʿAbdAllāh ق said many times, "Don't look at how I treat my family or you might fall in mistakes!" And we were the only ones passing through his door and then one day he called us and said, "Don't come in unless I call you." Mawlana Shaykh Nazim ق is teaching us; we are learning from him, so there should be no hard feelings as we all have mistakes, but we must look at our mistakes.

In *Madinah al-Munawwara,* Imam Malik ؓ had 600 teachers on *tasawwuf* and 300 teachers of Shariʿah and he never liked giving *fatwas,* saying, "This is dangerous because I might make a mistake." Look how much knowledge he has in his famous saying, "Whoever studied Sufism without *fiqh* is a heretic, and whoever studied *fiqh* without Sufism is corrupted, and whoever studied Sufism and *fiqh* will find the truth and reality of Islam."

Who does both will find reality! And yet with 600 teachers of *tasawwuf* and 300 teachers of *fiqh,* still he was afraid to give a *fatwa,* whereas today a child will give a *fatwa* from behind the computer, so you don't know if he is a child or old man. They merely collect some papers and type on different channels and it becomes a *fatwa.* Too many of Mawlana's *murīds* do that as well, and they argue with each other, "My Shaykh, your shaykh!" They don't even say, "Mawlana Shaykh Nazim ق said," but only, "My Shaykh said this and did this and he is better than your shaykh!" Who is your shaykh? They are all under Mawlana Shaykh's feet—all representatives, all deputies—everyone is under his feet as his *barakah* is on everyone!

Imam Shafiʿī ؓ had a Shaykh named Shaybān ar-Raʿī ؓ, and Imam Aḥmad bin Hanbal ؓ got upset with Imam Shafiʿī, saying, "You are an *imam!* How can you have Shaybān ar-Raʿī as your shaykh? How can you accept this?" as Shaybān ar-Raʿī ؓ was a scholar, but not of the rank of Imam Shafiʿī. So Imam Shafiʿī said many times to Imam Aḥmad, "Don't say that, please be careful and just leave it alone." Imam Shaybān ar-Ra'ī visited Imam Shafiʿī and when he made *wudu,* Imam Shafiʿī drank the cast-off *wudu* water. The Prophet ﷺ said that is bad water, as it takes all sins with it, so keep doing *wudu* and all your sins will be gone.

Imam Aḥmad ؓ could not accept Imam Shafiʿī ؓ doing that, as it is a basic principle in Shariʿah that the cast-off *wudu* water is dead, but Imam

Shafi'ī drank it, dead or not, as he knew the *barakah* of water that touched the *wali's* hands, feet and face. Where did those feet walk? Perhaps that *wali* walked in Paradise as *awlīyāullāh* are always in the Way of Allāh making *da'wa*. So once Shaykh Shaybān ar-Ra'ī ؏ came and Imam Aḥmad ؏ said, "I am going to ask him a question."

Imam Shafi'ī said, "No don't ask him, he will humiliate you. Don't ask him any questions!"

He said, "No, I am going to ask him a question." And he said, "*Yā* Shaybān. When you pray and say '*Allāhu Akbar*,' where do your thoughts mostly go?" When we pray, most often every thought of *dunya* comes to us and nothing comes from *Akhirah*, only Shayṭan comes.

Imam Shaybān ؏ looked at him and said, "O! I thought you were an *imam*, but it is better for you to go back home and pray all your prayers from the beginning, because all your prayers are not accepted." Imam Shafi'ī ؏ said "Didn't I tell you not to argue with him?" Then Imam Shaybān said, "O Imam Aḥmad! A child will not ask this question, so is there anything but Allāh's House in your heart to think about? Go and redo all your prayers from the day you became mature up to today!"

Imams guide us; if you don't have an authority on you, this is the authority and the other, the '*dunya* authority' is your country. We live in western countries and have to uphold their laws and love these countries because we live in them.

For example, so many generations of Muslims were born in England that they don't accept but to say, "I am English." If you are not English, why do you carry their passport? If you don't like it then go back to your country, Pakistan or wherever. When you carry that passport you are making a pledge to be a citizen. That applies to all countries in the west including America and Europe: if you are not happy, go home. But don't be like someone who takes water from a well and then throws stones in it to close it. No, be fair as Islam is fair to everyone.

Awlīyāullāh teach us how to love each other. The Prophet ﷺ said:

يحشر المرء مع من أحب

Yuhshar al-maruw ma' man ahab.

Each person will be resurrected with the one he loves.

If you love me you will be with me; if you love the Prophet ﷺ you will be with the Prophet ﷺ. And as people love the Prophet ﷺ, do you think that when they are resurrected with him that they will be in groups? Won't they be shy to be in groups, as they all love the Prophet ﷺ but they don't love each other? Are they going to say, "I want to be away from that one!" No, we will all be with the Prophet ﷺ. Therefore, imagine the Greatness of Sayyīdinā Muḥammad ﷺ on the Day of Judgment, he will be with everyone shoulder to shoulder! Doesn't the question 'how' come to your mind? He will be with everyone shoulder to shoulder until he takes them to their places in Paradise! Allāh ﷻ will give him the power to be with everyone in every moment, which is beyond our understanding, and to take the whole *ummah* to Paradise in such a way will only take less than a moment for him.

I was watching something today on the Internet and on TV that surprised and shocked me. Many people who are famous in religion have their own cable channels on which they speak about Islam, but it struck me to see this particular channel. For the first time I am seeing this person whose knowledge I respect sitting with very made-up women, very modern, blonde hair, singing and clapping their hands. I said, "What is this? Is this *ṭarīqah*? Is this the way we have to follow?" This man has lots of books and is very famous. Is this a way for him to please his government, for them to say he is modern? Or perhaps that is Paradise? I don't know.

So may Allāh ﷻ forgive him and forgive us. We are not better than him, but I brought this up to say that even to that extent, if he says "*astaghfirullāh*" and makes *wudu*, that will be enough to clear that, as Allāh ﷻ said:

إن رحمتي سبقت غضبي

Inna raḥmatī sabaqat ghadabī.

My Mercy precedes (outweighs) My Anger. (*Ḥadīth Qudsī*)

وَرَحْمَتِي وَسِعَتْ كُلَّ شَيْءٍ

Wa raḥmatī wasi'at kulla shay.

My Mercy has encompassed everything. (Sūrat al-A'rāf, 7:156)

O Muslims! Be happy, but not like that. Be happy by making more and more *ṣalawāt*, praise of the Prophet ﷺ and all messengers and by reading *Sūrat al-Fātiḥah* as much as you can.

May Allāh ﷻ forgive us and may Allāh ﷻ bless us.

Wa min Allāhi 't-tawfīq, bi ḥurmati 'l-ḥabīb, bi ḥurmati 'l-Fātiḥah.

And with Allāh is success. For the sake of the Beloved, for his sake we recite the opening chapter of Holy Qur'an.

Islamic Calendar and Holy Days

The Islamic calendar is lunar based, with twelve months of 29 or 30 days. A lunar year is shorter than a solar year, so Muslim holy days cycle back in the Gregorian (Western) calendar. This is how Ramaḍān is celebrated at different times of the year, as the annual Islamic calendar is ten days shorter than the Gregorian calendar.

Four Islamic months are sacred: Muharram, Rajab, Dhūl-Qʿadah and Dhūl-Hijjah. Holy months include "God's Month" (Rajab), "Prophet's Month" (Shaʿbān) and the "Month of the People" (Ramaḍān), in which pious acts are rewarded more generously.

Months of the Islamic Calendar

Muḥarram
Safar
Rabīʿ ul-Awwal (Rabīʿ I)
Rabīʿ uth-Thāni (Rabīʿ II)
Jumāda al-Awwal (Jumādi I)
Jumāda uth-Thāni (Jumādi II)
Rajab
Shaʿbān
Ramaḍān
Shawwāl
Dhū'l-Qʿadah
Dhū'l-Hijjah

al-Hijrah

The 1st of Muharram marks the beginning of the Islamic New Year, chosen because it is the anniversary of Prophet Muḥammad's ﷺ historic *hijrah* (migration) from Mecca to Madinah, where he established the first, preeminent Muslim community in which he introduced unprecedented social reforms, including civil law, human and women's rights, religious tolerance, taxation to serve the community, and military ethics.

'Ashura

On 10th Muharram, ʿAshūra commemorates many sacred events, such as Noah's ark coming to rest, the birth of Abraham, and the building of the Kaʿbah in Mecca. ʿAshūra is a major holy day, marked with two days of fasting, on the $9^{th}/10^{th}$ or on $10^{th}/11^{th}$ based on a holy tradition (*hadīth*) of Sayyīdinā Muḥammad ﷺ.

Mawlid

Mawlid al-Nabī, 12th Rabiʿ al-Awwal, commemorates Prophet Muḥammad's birth in 570. Mawlid is celebrated globally throughout this month in huge communal gatherings in which a famous poem "Qasīdah al-Burdah" is recited, accompanied by drummers, illustrious poetry recitals, religious singing, eloquent sermons, gift giving, feasts, and feeding the poor. Most Muslim nations observe Mawlid as a national holiday.

Laylat al-Isra wal-Mi'raj

Literally, "the Night Journey and Ascension;" 27th of Rajab is when Sayyīdinā Muḥammad ﷺ physically traveled from Mecca to Jerusalem, ascended in all the levels of Heaven from a rock in the Dome of the Rock, and returned to Mecca—while his bed was still warm. In the Night Journey, Islam's five daily prayers were ordained by God. Sayyīdinā Muḥammad ﷺ also prayed with Abraham, Moses, and Jesus in Jerusalem's al-Aqsa Mosque, signifying that Muslims, Christians, and Jews follow one god. This holy event designated Jerusalem as the third holiest site in Islam, after Mecca and Madinah.

Laylat al-Bara'ah

The "Night of Freedom from Fire" occurs on 15th Shaʿbān. On this night God's Mercy is great; hence, the night is spent reciting Holy Qurʿan and special prayers, as well as visiting the deceased.

Ramadan

Many regard Ramaḍān, the 9th month of the Islamic calendar, the holiest month of the year. Muslims observe a strict fast and participate in pious activities such as charitable giving and peace making. It is a time of intense spiritual renewal for those who observe it. Fasting is meant to instill social awareness of the needy, and to promote gratitude for God's endless favors. The fast is typically broken in a communal setting, and hence Ramaḍān is a highly social month. At night, a special Ramaḍān prayer known as "Tarawīh" is offered in congregation, in which one-thirtieth of the Holy Qurʿan is recited by the *imām* (prayer leader); thus the entire holy book of 6,000 verses is recited in this month.

Eid al-Fitr

"Festival of Fast-Breaking" marks the end of Ramaḍān and is celebrated the first three days of Shawwāl. It is a time for charity and celebration with family and friends for completing a month of blessings and joy. In the Last Days of Ramaḍān, each Muslim family gives "Zakāt al-Fitr"(charity of fast-breaking) which consists of cash and/or food, to help the poor. On the first early morning of Eid, Muslims observe a special congregational prayer, such as Christmas/Easter Mass or the High Holy Days. After Eid prayer is a time to visit family and friends, and give gifts and money (especially to children). Many specialty foods and sweets are prepared solely for Eid days. In most Muslim countries, the entire three days of Eid is a national holiday.

Yawm al-Arafat

"Day of ʿArafat," the 9th Dhul-Hijjah, occurs just before the celebration of Eid al-Adha. Pilgrims on *Sunnah* assemble for the "standing" on the plain of ʿArafat, located outside Mecca, where they contemplate the Day of Standing (Resurrection Day). Muslims elsewhere in the world fast this day, and gather at a local mosque for prayers. Thus, those who cannot perform *Sunnah* that year still honor the sacrifice of Abraham.

Eid al-Adha

The "Feast of Sacrifice," celebrated from the 10th-13th Dhul-Hijjah, marks Prophet Abraham's willingness to sacrifice his son Ismāʿīl on God's order. To honor this event, Muslims perform *Sunnah,* the pilgrimage to Mecca that is incumbent on every mature Muslim once in their life if they have the means. Celebrations begin with an animal sacrifice to commemorate Sayyīdinā Abraham's sacrifice. In Islam, he is known as *Khalilullāh,* "God's friend." Many consider him the first Muslim and a premiere role model, for his obedience to God and willingness to sacrifice his only child without even questioning the command.

Glossary

ʿabd (pl. *ʿibād*): lit. slave; servant.
ʿAbdAllāh: Lit., "servant of God"
Abū Bakr aṣ-Ṣiddīq: the closest Companion of Prophet Muḥammad; the Prophet's father-in-law, who shared the *Hijrah* with him. After the Prophet's death, he was elected the first caliph (successor); known as one of the most saintly Companions.
Abū Yazīd/Bayāzīd Bistāmī: A great ninth century *walī* and a master of the Naqshbandi Golden Chain.
adab: good manners, proper etiquette.
adhān: call to prayer.
Ākhirah: the Hereafter; afterlife.
al-: Arabic definite article, "the".
ʿalāmīn: world; universes.
Alḥamdūlillāh: praise God.
ʿAlī ibn Abī Ṭālib: first cousin of Prophet Muḥammad, married to his daughter Fāṭimah; the fourth caliph.
alif: first letter of Arabic alphabet.
ʿAlīm, al-: the Knower, a divine attribute
Allāh: proper name for God in Arabic.
Allāhu Akbar: God is Greater.
ʿāmal: good deed (pl. *ʿamāl*).
amīr (pl., *umarā*): chief, leader, head of a nation or people.
anā: first person singular pronoun
anbīyā: prophets (sing. *nabī*).
ʿaql: intellect, reason; from the root *ʿaqila*: lit., "to fetter."
ʿArafah, ʿArafat: a plain near Mecca where pilgrims gather for the principal rite of *Hajj*.
ʿarif: knower, Gnostic; one who has reached spiritual knowledge of his Lord.
ʿĀrifūnʿ bil-Lāh: knowers of God.
Ar-Raḥīm: The Mercy-Giving, Merciful, Munificent, one of Allāh's ninety-nine Holy Names.
Ar-Raḥmān: The Most Merciful, Compassionate, Beneficent; the most repeated of Allāh's Holy Names.
ʿarsh, al-: the Divine Throne.
aṣl: root, origin, basis.
astāghfirullāh: lit. "I seek Allāh's forgiveness."
Awlīyāullāh: saints of Allāh (sing. *walī*).
āyah (pl. *ayāt*): a verse of the Holy Qur'an.
Āyat al-Kursī: "Verse of the Throne," a well-known supplication from the Qur'an (2:255).
ʿAzraʾīl: the Archangel of Death.
Badīʿ al-: The Innovator; a divine name.
Banī Ādam: Children of Adam; humanity.
Bayt al-Maqdis: the Sacred Mosque in Jerusalem, built at the site where Solomon's Temple was later erected.
Bayt al-Māʾmūr: much-frequented house; this refers to the Kaʿbah of the Heavens, which is the prototype of the Kaʿbah on Earth, circumambulated by the angels.
bayaʿ: pledge; in the context of this book, the pledge of initiation of a disciple (*murīd*) to a Shaykh.
Bismillāhi'r-Raḥmāni'r-Raḥīm: "In the name of the All-Merciful, the All-Compassionate"; introductory verse to all chapters of the Qur'an, except the ninth.

Dajjāl: the False Messiah (Anti-Christ) will appear at the end-time of this world, to deceive Mankind with false divinity.
dalālah: evidence.
dhāt: self / selfhood.
dhawq (pl. *adhwāq*): tasting; technical term referring to the experiential aspect of gnosis.
dhikr: remembrance, mention of God in His Holy Names or phrases of glorification.
ḍīyā: light.
Diwān al-Awlīyā: the nightly gathering of saints with Prophet Muḥammad in the spiritual realm.
du'ā: supplication.
dunyā: world; worldly life.
'Eid: festival; the two major celebrations of Islam are 'Eid al-Fitr, after Ramaḍān; and 'Eid al-Adha, the Festival of Sacrifice during the time of *Hajj*, which commemorates the sacrifice of Prophet Abraham.
farḍ: obligatory worship.
Fātiḥah: Sūratu 'l-Fātiḥah; the opening chapter of the Qur'an.
Ghafūr, al-: The Forgiver; one of the Holy Names of God.
ghawth: lit. "Helper"; the highest rank of all saints.
ghaybu' l-muṭlaq, al-: the Absolute Unknown; known only to God.
ghusl: full shower/bath obligated by a state of ritual impurity, performed before worship.
Grandshaykh: generally, a *walī* of great stature. In this text, refers to Mawlana 'AbdAllāh ad-Daghestāni (d. 1973), Mawlana Shaykh Nazim's master.
hā': the Arabic letter ه
ḥadīth Nabawī (pl., *aḥadīth*): prophetic *ḥadīth* whose meaning and linguistic expression are those of Prophet Muḥammad.
Ḥadīth Qudsī: divine saying whose meaning directly reflects the meaning God intended but whose linguistic expression is not divine speech as in the Qur'an.
ḥaḍr: present
Hajj: the sacred pilgrimage of Islam obligatory on every mature Muslim once in their life.
ḥalāl: permitted, lawful according to Islamic *Sharī'ah*.
ḥaqīqah, al-: reality of existence; ultimate truth.
ḥaqq: truth
Ḥaqq, al-: the Divine Reality, one of the 99 Divine Names.
ḥarām: forbidden, unlawful.
ḥasanāt: good deeds.
hāshā: God forbid.
ḥarf: (pl. *ḥurūf*) letter; Arabic root "edge."
Ḥawā: Eve.
ḥaywān: animal.
Hijrah: emigration.
ḥikmah: wisdom.
ḥujjah: proof.
hūwa: the pronoun "he,"made up of the Arabic letters *hā'* and *wāw*.
'ibādu 'l-Lāh: servants of God.
'ifrīt: a type of Jinn, huge and powerful.
iḥsān: doing good, "It is to worship God as though you see Him; for if you are not seeing Him, He sees you."
ikhlāṣ, al-: sincere devotion.
ilāh: (pl. *āliha*): idols or gods.
ilāhīyya: divinity.

ilhām: divine inspiration sent to *awlīyāullāh*.
ʿilm: knowledge, science.
ʿilmu ʾl-awrāq: knowledge of papers.
ʿilmu ʾl-adhwāq: knowledge of taste.
ʿilmu ʾl-ḥurūf: science of letters.
ʿilmu ʾl-kalām: scholastic theology.
ʿilmun ladunnī: divinely inspired knowledge.
imān: faith, belief.
imām: leader of congregational prayer; an advanced scholar followed by a large community.
insān: humanity; pupil of the eye.
insānu ʾl-kāmil, al-: the Perfect Man, *i.e.*, Prophet Muḥammad.
irādatullāh: the Will of God.
irshād: spiritual guidance.
ism: name.
isma-Llāh: name of God.
isrāʿ: night journey; used here in reference to the night journey of Prophet Muḥammad.
Isrāʿfīl: Archangel Rafael, in charge of blowing the Final Trumpet.
jalāl: majesty.
jamāl: beauty.
jamaʿa: group, congregation.
Jannah: Paradise.
jihād: to struggle in God's Path.
Jibrīl: Gabriel, Archangel of revelation.
Jinn: a species of living beings created from fire, invisible to most humans. Jinn can be Muslims or non-Muslims.
Jumuʿah: Friday congregational prayer, held in a large mosque.
Kaʿbah: the first House of God, located in Mecca, Saudi Arabia to which pilgrimage is made and to which Muslims face in prayer.
kāfir: unbeliever.
Kalāmullāh al-Qadīm: lit., Allāh's Ancient Words, *viz.* the Holy Qur'an.
kalīmat at-tawḥīd: lā ilāha illa-Llāh: "There is no god but Al-Lah (the God)."
karāmat: miracles.
khalīfah: deputy.
Khāliq, al-: the Creator, one of 99 Divine Names.
khalq: Creation.
khāniqah: designated smaller place for worship other than a mosque; *zāwiyah*.
khuluq: conduct, manners.
Kirāmun Kātabīn: honored Scribe angels.
lā: no; not; not existent; the particle of negation.
lā ilāha illa-Llāh Muḥammadun Rasūlullāh: There is no deity except Allāh, Muḥammad is the Messenger of Allāh.
lām: Arabic letter ل.
al-Lawḥ al-Maḥfūẓ: the Preserved Tablets.
Laylat al-Isrāʿ wa'l-Miʿrāj: the Night Journey and Ascension of Prophet Muḥammad to Jerusalem and to the Seven Heavens.
Madīnātu ʾl-Munawwara: the Illuminated city; city of Prophet Muḥammad; Madinah.
mahr: dowry, given by the groom to the bride.
malakūt: divine kingdom.
Malik, al-: the Sovereign, a divine name.
Mālik: Archangel of Hell.
maqām: spiritual station; tomb of a prophet, messenger or saint.
maʿrifah: gnosis.
Māshā'Allāh: as Allāh Wills.

Mawlānā: lit. "Our master" or "our patron,"referring to an esteemed person.
maẓhar: place of disclosure.
miḥrāb: prayer niche.
Mikāʿīl: Michael, Archangel of rain.
mīzān: the scale that weighs our deeds on Judgment Day.
mīm: Arabic letter م.
minbar: pulpit.
Miracles: of saints, known as *karamāt*; of prophets, known as *muʿjizāt* (lit., "That which renders powerless or helpless").
miʿrāj: the ascension of Prophet Muḥammad from Jerusalem to the Seven Heavens.
Muḥammadun rasūlu ʾl-Lāh: Muḥammad is the Messenger of God.
mulk, al-: the World of dominion.
Muʿmin, al-: Guarḍian of Faith, one of the 99 Names of God.
muʿmin: a believer.
munājāt: invocation to God in a very intimate form.
Munkir: one of the angels of the grave.
murīd: disciple, student, follower.
murshid: spiritual guide; *pir*.
mushāhadah: direct witnessing.
mushrik (pl. *mushrikūn*): idolater; polytheist.
muwwāḥid (pl. *muwāḥḥidūn*): those who affirm God's Oneness.
nabī: a prophet of God.
nāfs: lower self, ego.
Nakīr: the other angel of the grave (with Munkir).
nūr: light.
Nūḥ: the prophet Noah.
Nūr, an-: "The Source of Light"; a divine name.
Qādir, al-: "The Powerful"; a divine name.
qalam, al-: the Pen.
qiblah: direction, specifically, the direction faced by Muslims during prayer and other worship, towards the Sacred House in Mecca.
Quddūs, al-: "The Holy One"; a divine name.
qurb: nearness
quṭb (pl. *aqṭāb*): axis or pole. Among the poles are:
Quṭbu ʾl-Bilād: Pole of the Lands.
Quṭbu ʾl-Irshād: Pole of Guidance.
Quṭbu ʾl-Aqṭāb: Pole of Poles.
Quṭbu ʾl-Aʿdham: Highest Pole.
Quṭbu ʾl-Mutaṣarrif: Pole of Affairs.
al-quṭbīyyatu ʾl-kubrā: the highest station of poleship.
Rabb, ar-: the Lord.
Raḥīm, ar-: "The Most Compassionate"; a divine name.
Raḥmān, ar-: "The All-Merciful"; a divine name.
raḥmā: mercy.
rakaʿat: one full set of prescribed motions in prayer. Each prayer consists of a one or more *rakaʿats.*
Ramaḍān: the ninth month of the Islamic calendar; month of fasting.
Rasūl: a messenger of God.
Rasūlullāh: the Messenger of God, Muḥammad ﷺ.
Raʿūf, ar-: "The Most Kind"; a divine name.
Razzāq, ar-: "The Provider"; a divine name.
rawḥānīyyah: spirituality; spiritual essence of something.
Riḍwān: Archangel of Paradise.
rizq: provision; sustenance.

rūḥ: spirit. *Ar-Rūḥ* is the name of a great angel.
rukūʿ: bowing posture of the prayer.
ṣadaqah: voluntary charity.
Ṣaḥābah (sing., *ṣaḥābī*): Companions of the Prophet; the first Muslims.
ṣaḥīḥ: authentic; term certifying validity of a *ḥadīth* of the Prophet.
ṣāim: fasting person (pl. *ṣāimūn*)
sajda (pl. *sujūd*): prostration.
ṣalāt: ritual prayer, one of the five obligatory pillars of Islam. Also, to invoke blessing on the Prophet.
Ṣalāt an-Najāt: prayer of salvation, offered in the late hours of night.
ṣalawāt (sing. *ṣalāt*): invoking blessings and peace upon the Prophet.
salām: peace.
Salām, as-: "The Peaceful"; a divine name. *As-salāmu ʿalaykum:* "Peace be upon you," the Islamic greeting.
Ṣamad, aṣ-: Self-Sufficient, upon whom creatures depend.
ṣawm, ṣiyām: fasting.
sayyi'āt: bad deeds; sins.
sayyid: leader; also, a descendant of Prophet Muḥammad.
Sayyīdinā: our master (fem. *sayyidunā; sayyidatunā*: our mistress).
shahādah: lit. testimony; the testimony of Islamic faith: *lā ilāha illa ʾl-Lāh wa Muḥammadun rasūlu ʾl-Lāh,* "There is no god but Allāh, the One God, and Muḥammad is the Messenger of God."
Shah Naqshband: Muḥammad Bahauddin Shah Naqshband, a great eighth century walī, and the founder of the Naqshbandi Ṭarīqah.
Shaykh: lit. "old Man," a religious guide, teacher; master of spiritual discipline.
shifāʿ: cure.
shirk: polytheism, idolatry, ascribing partners to God
ṣiffāt: attributes; term referring to Divine Attributes.
Silsilat adh-dhahabīyya: "Golden Chain"of spiritual authority in Islam
sohbet (Arabic, *suḥbah*): association: the assembly or discourse of a Shaykh.
subḥānAllāh: glory be to God.
sulṭān/sulṭānah: ruler, monarch.
Sulṭān al-Awlīyā: lit., "King of the *awlīyā*; the highest-ranking saint.
Sūnnah: Practices of Prophet Muḥammad in actions and words; what he did, said, recommended, or approved of in his Companions.
sūrah: a chapter of the Qur'an; picture, image.
Sūratu ʾl-Ikhlāṣ: Chapter 114 of Holy Qur'an; the Chapter of Sincerity.
ṭabīb: doctor.
tābiʿīn: the Successors, one generation after the Prophet's Companions.
tafsīr: to explain, expound, explicate, or interpret; technical term for commentary or exegesis of the Holy Qur'an.
tajallī (pl. *tajallīyāt*): theophanies, God's self-disclosures, Divine Self-manifestation.
takbīr: lit. *"Allāhu Akbar,"*God is Great.
tarawīḥ: the special nightly prayers of Ramaḍān.
ṭarīqat/ṭarīqah: lit., way, road or path. An Islamic order or path of discipline

and devotion under a guide or Shaykh; Sufism.
taṣbīḥ: recitation glorifying or praising God.
tawāḍaʿ: humbleness.
ṭawāf: the rite of circumambulating the Kaʿbah while glorifying God during *Hajj* and ʿUmra.
tawḥīd: unity; universal or primordial Islam, submission to God, as the sole Master of destiny and ultimate Reality.
Tawrāt: Torah
tayammum: Alternate ritual ablution performed in the absence of water.
ʿubūdīyyah: state of worshipfulness. Servanthood
ʿulamā (sing. *ʿālim*): scholars.
ʿulūmu ʾl-awwalīna wa ʾl-ākhirīn: knowledge of the "Firsts"and the "Lasts" refers to the knowledge God poured into the heart of Prophet Muḥammad during his ascension to the Divine Presence.
ʿulūm al-Islāmī: Islamic religious sciences.
Ummāh: faith community, nation.
ʿUmar ibn al-Khaṭṭāb: an eminent Companion of Prophet Muḥammad and second caliph of Islam.
ʿumra: the minor pilgrimage to Mecca, performed at any time of the year.
ʿUthmān ibn ʿAffān: eminent Companion of the Prophet; his son-in-law and third caliph of Islam, renowned for compiling the Qur'an.
walad: a child.
waladī: my child.
walāyah: proximity or closeness; sainthood.
walī (pl. *awlīyā*): saint, or "he who assists"; guarḍian; protector.
wasīlah: a means; holy station of Prophet Muḥammad as God's intermediary to grant supplications.
wāw: Arabic letter و
wujūd, al-: existence; "to find," "the act of finding," and "being found."
Yʿaqūb: Jacob; the prophet.
yamīn: the right hand; previously meant "oath."
Yawm al-ʿahdi waʾl-mīthāq: Day of Oath and Covenant, a heavenly event before this Life, when all souls of humanity were present to God, and He took from each the promise to accept His Sovereignty as Lord.
yawm al-qiyāmah: Day of Judgment.
Yūsuf: Joseph; the prophet.
zāwiyah: designated smaller place for worship other than a mosque; also *khāniqah*.
zīyāra: visitation to the grave of a prophet, a prophet's companion or a saint.

Other Publications (available at www.isn1.net)

Shaykh Muhammad Nazim Adil al-Haqqani

- We Have Honored the Children of Adam (2013)
- Heavenly Counsel: from Darkness into Light (2013)
- In the Mystic Footsteps of Saints (eBooks) (2) (2013)
- Heavenly Showers (2012)
- The Sufilive Series (6) (2010-12)
- Breaths from Beyond the Curtain
- In the Eye of the Needle
- Eternity: Inspirations from Heavenly Sources
- The Healing Power of Sufi Meditation
- In the Mystic Footsteps of Saints (2)
- Liberating the Soul (6)

Shaykh Muḥammad Hisham Kabbani

- The Hierarchy of Saints (2013)
- The Heavenly Power of Divine Obedience and Gratitude (2013)
- Salawat of Tremendous Blessings (*also Turkish/ Spanish*)
- The Dome of Provisions (2012)
- The Prohibition of Domestic Violence in Islam (2011)
- The Sufilive Series (6 vol. 2010-2012)
- Jihad: Principles of Leadership in War and Peace
- Cyprus Summer Series (2 vol.)
- The Nine-fold Ascent
- Who Are the Guides? (2008)
- Illuminations (2007)
- Banquet for the Soul (2006)
- Symphony of Remembrance
- The Healing Power of Sufi Meditation
- In the Shadow of Saints
- Keys to the Divine Kingdom
- The Sufi Science of Self-Realization (*also in French*)
- Universe Rising: the Approach of Armageddon?
- Pearls and Coral
- Classical Islam and the Naqshbandi Sufi Tradition
- The Naqshbandi Sufi Way
- Links of Light: The Golden Chain
- Encyclopedia of Islamic Doctrine (7 volumes)
- Angels Unveiled, a Sufi Perspective
- Encyclopedia of Muḥammad's Women Companions and the Traditions They Related

Hajjah Amina Adil

- Muḥammad: the Messenger of Islam (2001)
- The Light of Muḥammad
- Lore of Light / Links of Light
- My Little Lore of Light (3 vol.)

Hajjah Naziha Adil Kabbani

- Heavenly Foods (2011)
- Secrets of Heavenly Food (2009)

www.ingramcontent.com/pod-product-compliance
Lightning Source LLC
Chambersburg PA
CBHW020415080526
44584CB00014B/1338
* 9 7 8 1 9 3 0 4 0 9 8 9 7 *